PROCEEDINGS OF THE CONVENTION

OF THE

REPUBLICAN PARTY

OF LOUISIANA,

HELD AT ECONOMY HALL, NEW ORLEANS, SEPTEMBER 25, 1865,

AND OF THE

CENTRAL EXECUTIVE COMMITTEE

OF THE

FRIENDS OF UNIVERSAL SUFFRAGE OF LOUISIANA

NOW,

"THE CENTRAL EXECUTIVE COMMITTEE OF THE
REPUBLICAN PARTY OF LOUISIANA."

Published by Left of Brain Books

Copyright © 2021 Left of Brain Books

ISBN 978-1-396-31877-1

First Edition

All rights reserved. No part of this publication may be reproduced, distributed, or transmitted in any form or by any means, including photocopying, recording, or other electronic or mechanical methods, without the prior written permission of the publisher, except in the case of brief quotations embodied in critical reviews and certain other noncommercial uses permitted by copyright law. Left of Brain Books is a division of Left of Brain Onboarding Pty Ltd.

Table of Contents

INTRODUCTION.

This pamphlet has been compiled in pursuance of a resolution of the Convention of the *"Republican Party of Louisiana,"* and of the *"Central Executive Committee of the Friends of Universal Suffrage of Louisiana,"* now the *"Central Executive Committee of the Republican Party."*

It comprises the most important of the proceedings of the "Committee" and Convention, and it is believed will be found to contain much that is not only highly interesting, but useful and important information to all who have the true interests of the rights and privileges of citizens at heart.

Within the boundaries of Louisiana are three hundred thousand citizens, who, until made *Freemen* by the *"Emancipation Proclamation"* of President *Lincoln*, were held in the bonds of slavery. Their owners were declared to be in a state of insurrection, disloyal to the Government, committing the greatest of all crimes, that of treason to the mildest and most beneficent government that has ever existed.

These late owners of nearly one-half of the population still claim the authority to govern the whole, excluding the three hundred thousand emancipated and loyal citizens from taking any part in the government; thus subverting the first principles of a republican form of government — the right of representation.

A few loyal citizens, inspired by the same spirit of liberty and the rights of man that actuated our forefathers, the first patriots of our country, to organize the government under which the people have enjoyed more prosperity and happiness than the people of any other nation, either ancient or modern, have organized the party whose proceedings are detailed in these pages.

They now call upon all citizens and friends of liberty to aid them in the important work of obtaining for all, of whatever race or color, equal rights and privileges — that all may be represented in the halls of legislation in the State, and in the Congress of the United States — that all may be equally entitled to represent and to be represented, to become electors, to vote and to be voted for; in a word, to be entitled to all the rights and privileges of citizenship, including the right of suffrage.

The battle of bullets has been fought and the Union has gained the victory. The battle of ballots has commenced and will surely gain the victory, but may take a little more time. It will as surely win, because the cause is just, and because the strong arm of the *Almighty Ruler of nations* will aid the arms of the just in obtaining the victory.

The emancipated and unenfranchised citizens will find in these pages much that is designed to aid them in obtaining their political rights. They should read it whenever and wherever it may fall into their hands. Those who can read, should read and explain the object of it to their emancipated brethren who cannot.

The "*Republican Party of Louisiana*" is the first and only organized party that has earnestly adopted the cause of the unenfranchised, and will not lay down its arms until the object is attained.

These citizens, in every parish and on every plantation, should organize associations and clubs, in accordance with the "Republican Party of Louisiana," and immediately open correspondence, addressing their communications to the Corresponding Secretary, at 49 Union street, New Orleans. They are advised to subscribe to the New Orleans Tribune, in the columns of which paper they will find the important proceedings of the party, as well as much other matter that will interest them; and also all the important news of the times.

Emancipated and unenfranchised citizens, you are three hundred thousand, and the enfranchised are three hundred and fifty thousand. You have, therefore, but to claim and obtain your rights of citizenship, and to make friends of twenty-six thousand of the enfranchised, when you will not only enjoy the blessings of Freedom, but will also have a majority, participating in the richest and best of all political blessings, that of choosing who you will have to make the laws under which you will live, and love to obey. You will then, and not until then, become truly republican citizens, invested with all their rights and privileges, the greatest and best and most exalted of all the nations that exist.

CENTRAL EXECUTIVE COMMITTEE
OF THE FRIENDS OF UNIVERSAL SUFFRAGE,
OF LOUISIANA,
NEW ORLEANS, JUNE, 1865.

The following advertisement appeared in the New Orleans Tribune, in French and English.

NOTICE.
TO THE FRIENDS OF UNIVERSAL SUFFRAGE.

The Friends of Universal Suffrage, and of the New Orleans Tribune, are invited to meet at No. 49 Union street, between Carondelet and Baronne, on Saturday the 10th inst. (June 1865) at 7 ½ o'clock, in the evening.

Matters of the highest importance will be brought before the Meeting. Come one! Come all!

T.J. DURANT,
C.W. HORNOR,
W.R. CRANE,
A. FERNANDEZ.

In pursuance of the above call, a meeting of citizens was held at 49 Union street. The meeting was called to order by W.R. Crane, who moved that T.J. Durant be invited to take the chair, which was unanimously adopted.

On motion of W.R. Crane, Alfred Jervis was appointed Secretary.

On motion of W.R. Crane, it was resolved that a Committee be appointed by the chair, of seven persons, who shall report at an adjourned meeting, the names of six persons from each of the four municipal districts of the city of New Orleans, clothed and charged with all the executive duties of a Central Committee of the Friends of Universal Suffrage, in Louisiana, for the period of one year, from the first day of June 1865, with power to fill all vacancies that may happen, during the period for which the same are chosen, and to order the time, place and manner of electing another Committee for the succeeding year.

The chair then appointed the following Committee of Seven:

W.R. CRANE,	OSCAR J. DUNN,	ALFRED JERVIS
LOUIS BANKS,	HENRY TRAIN,	CLEMENT CAMP,
	ANSEL EDWARDS.	

Adjourned to Friday evening, June 16th, at 7 ½ o'clock.

In pursuance of adjournment, the Friends of Universal Suffrage met at 49 Union street. The President called the meeting to order, when W.R Crane, Chairman of the Committee of seven, appointed at the last meeting, submitted the following names to constitute the Central Executive Committee of the Friends of Universal Suffrage in Louisiana.

For First District.
THOMAS J. DURANT,
W.R. CRANE,
ANSEL EDWARDS,
CHARLES OGILVIE,
ALFRED JERVIS,
JOS. L. MONTIEU.

For Second District.
B. F. FLANDERS,
HENRY TRAIN,
ANTHONY FERNANDEZ,
SEBASTIAN SEILER,
ARNAUD COMMAGERE,
OSCAR J. DUNN.

For Third District.
JOHN McWHIRTER,
H. STILES,
J. L. IMLAY,
ROCH ABERTON,
J. B. DUPLAINE,
F. CHRISTOPHE.

For Fourth District.
RUFUS WAPLES,
A. H. WHITNEY,
R.W. STANLEY,
S. J. BROWER,
D. C. WOODRUFF,
JOSEPH P. JOHNSON.

The Report was approved and adopted unanimously.

W.R. Crane presented a resolution, that a voluntary registration of Citizens not recognized as voters be made.

On motion of C. W. Hornor, the resolution was referred to the Executive Committee. Adjourned.

In accordance with a notice published by the Chairman, the Committee met and proceeded to organize permanently by electing T.J. Durant, President, Anthony Fernandez, Vice-President and Alfred Jervis, Secretary.

On motion, the chair appointed a Committee of three, consisting of W.R. Crane, J. L. Montieu and S. Seiler, to report what other officers the Committee requires, and suitable persons to fill the same.

A Committee, on motion of Mr. O.J. Dunn, was appointed to prepare and report a platform of principles for the Central Executive Committee of the Friends of Universal Suffrage.

Mr. Crane moved to take up his resolutions relative to the registration of the citizens of color. This being agreed to, he supported them in a very able speech:

This registration is not intended for Louisiana, but for the National Congress. Agitation is growing up on this subject. The Executive by limitating the suffrage to one race has alarmed the friends of freedom. We propose to take the sense of the people, and to hold here an election, among the citizens of color, for Governor and for Representatives. I hope and trust the President may have been actuated by a fair sense of devotion to his duty. But before such a manifestation, he will change his policy, and set aside these Copperhead Governors who seek the support of the rebels.

I propose, therefore, that a candidate be chosen by the loyal party, in opposition to the Copperheads, in order to show that the entire vote of the colored population will be cast for a loyal man. And when the Copperhead elected by the white voters shall present himself to Congress, this will be an energetic protest. (Applause.)

The State has been reorganized by executive usurpation; the result is a state of anarchy. Reconstruction, so far, has been a failure. The Representative so elected will not be admitted as a member on the floor of Congress, but he will be received as a delegate of a territory, and will be heard as such in the Hall of Representatives. (Applause.)

But it remains to regulate the details. The Committee will have to secure a registration of the whole colored citizens. All other qualifications should be observed, except the clause "white." The friends of this movement, in the State and in the North, will gladly furnish the means for the execution of the plan.

Louisiana was intended to become the pillar of reconstruction. The prediction has not been fulfilled. But if we act as proposed, she will become the true pioneer, by having the first delegate upon the floor of Congress. She will be the pioneer in the work of reconstruction on the broad principle of the Declaration of Independence. If refused, it would follow that a whole race has no right to life, liberty and the pursuit of happiness, and that would be monstrous.

After alluding to the opinion of Justice Curtis, in the Dred Scott case, and to the refusal of the National Convention to insert the word "white" into the Federal Constitution, Mr. Crane concluded by an earnest appeal to combat the aristocracy, which was greeted with applause.

The future consideration of the subject was postponed until the next morning.

On motion of Mr. Train, a committee of three was appointed to draft an application to the Governor, asking for a registration of the colored citizens. The Chair appointed Messrs. Train, Imlay and Aberton.

June 29th, 1865.

The Committee met at the usual hour.

The Committee of three, to whom was referred the matter of appropriate officers, and recommend suitable persons to fill those for which persons have not already been elected, reported 1st: That the officers of the Committee shall consist of a President, Vice-President, Recording Secretary, Assistant Recording Secretary, Corresponding Secretary, Assistant Corresponding Secretary, and a Treasurer; and recommend for Treasurer, W.R. Crane; for Corresponding Secretary, H.C. Warmoth; for Assistant, Wm. Mulford; for Assistant Recording a Secretary, J.L. Montieu, who were all unanimously elected.

On motion of Mr. R. Waples, "The New Orleans Tribune" was declared the Official Organ of this Committee. Mr. Durant presented an address to the Governor on Registration, which was on motion adopted and signed by all the officers and members present; and a Committee of three consisting of

Messrs. Fernandez, Ogilvie and Crane, was appointed, to which was added the President, to present the address to the Governor. Hon. John Covode, of Pennsylvania, was then introduced by Mr. Durant.

Mr. Covode rose up amidst the general attention of the audience, and spoke substantially as follows:

SPEECH OF HONORABLE JOHN COVODE:

GENTLEMEN, you will not, of course, expect a speech from me; but I have a few words to say to encourage you in your efforts. I know the sentiment of Congress, and I feel perfectly sure that until the people of Louisiana adopt the policy advocated here tonight, no representatives of your State will ever be admitted on the floor of Congress. [Loud applause.] You may find obstacles in your way, you may be betrayed; but stand firm, gentlemen, and the loyal people of the nation will stand with you. [Renewed applause.]

I am glad I have come here. I came to be posted through personal observation on the state of affairs. I have seen the freedmen on the plantations. I am going back to Washington, well aware of the condition of things, and will have to report my views on the best policy for the Government to follow. My view is that all loyal men ought to vote. [Applause.] My view is that the struggle be not for nought. The disfranchised colored men would be in condition worse than before. I advise you to continue your policy. I will not detain you any longer; but without further remark, I will say that you are on the right track. [Loud applause.]

After Mr. Covode had taken his seat, the meeting adjourned.

July 6th, 1865.

The report of Mr. Dunn chairman of the Committee on Platform was read by the Secretary and adopted, as follows:

GENTLEMEN —Your Committee honored by the appointment to the important duty of setting forth to the world the true principles of this Association; beg leave to submit the following report:

On entering upon the duty of calling together the various elements that favor in this community the sacred principles of the Declaration of

Independence, the Central Executive Committee of the Friends of Universal Suffrage beg leave to address a few words to their fellow-citizens.

Our forefathers laid the base of practical democracy and of true republicanism, when they proclaimed to the land, in the most solemn hour of the American History: "We hold these truths to be self-evident — that all men are created equal; that they are endowed by their Creator with certain inalienable rights that among these are life, liberty and the pursuit of happiness; that to secure these rights, governments are instituted among men, deriving their just powers from the consent of the governed."

Taking this broad platform as the true expression of republican principles, we have only to follow the consequences, in order to set forth before the people of Louisiana the spirit of our Association.

All men are created equal. It is the beast and the glory of the American Republic that there is no discrimination among men, no privileges founded upon birth-right. There are no hereditary distinctions; nobility is unknown; not a single public office is transmitted from father to son, not even the highest office in the empire — this country being a republic and not a monarchy. Every career, every pursuit in life is open to the humblest as well as to the most exalted citizen. So little is the importance of birth considered, that a self-made man is viewed with more esteem and respect than the citizen born and raised in affluence and prosperity.

Our country is, therefore, one of republican ideas and republican manners. The chance or the contingencies of birth have no power in America. A man is not what his name and his extraction have made him; he is what he makes himself. Nobody would consent to have any career open only to the descendants of certain families and shut up to the balance of the citizens.

All discrimination on account of birth or origin is, therefore, repugnant to the principles of our Government and to American manners and customs themselves. It is true that one, only one discrimination of that kind remains — that having the effect of prescribing the African race. But as long as slavery existed in the land, color was taken for a characteristic of servitude, and thereby the African race was enveloped in a law of proscription. Now, slavery is no more. On the proud land of the United States, we no longer know anything but freemen. And the principle of, equality of men has to bring forth its full consequence, unless that principle itself be jeopardized. The American

State Constitutions have to be consistent with the republican manners of the people, unless they open the door for the institution of aristocracy, nobility, an even monarchy.

We, therefore, deprecate any discrimination founded upon origin or birth. We deprecate any inquiry into the extraction of citizens. We want that all be given a fair chance in the world, with the same rights before the law; that each one be free and unobstructed to find his own level, according to his education and means.

Moreover, it will be to the honor of the great republic that the inalienable rights, conferred by the Creator upon all members of the human family, be actually respected in all citizens. If life, liberty and the pursuit of happiness are rights which belong to all men, let all men enjoy them. After having blotted out from the starry banner of the Union the dark spot of slavery, with the stocks, the manacles, the whip, and torture, shall we say that four or five millions of our countrymen, four or five millions of freemen have no right to life, liberty and the pursuit of happiness? For none of these can be secured without enjoying political rights. Life is insecure when the proscribed race has no voice in the legislative hall, and no friend in the jury-box. Liberty is but a word as long as taxation, elections, and the whole political machinery are confined in the hands of an inimical race. Happiness itself, which, according to a great philosopher, is the aim of all living creatures, cannot be attained without adequate protection and justice to the individual.

Therefore, let our republican government be upheld by all citizens and derive its just power from the expressed consent of ALL governed. Being just it will feel stronger; resting on the base of Universal Suffrage, it will be an example set to the world.

The political campaign we are entering upon will have no ordinary importance. We have set forth our views. We make an earnest appeal to our fellow citizens to join us fighting this last battle, that will settle the vexed question forever.

Being consistent, by being just, by being great, the people of the United States will insure their future happiness for long years to come, and gain the admiration of all civilized nations.

OSCAR J. DUNN,
Chairman of the Committee.

New Orleans, June 29, 1865.

Mr. Durant, in behalf of the committee appointed to wait upon Governor Wells, stated that the Governor did not think fit to reply in the same manner that he had been addressed, that is to say in writing. His reply appeared in the evening papers, two days ago. Under this circumstance, Mr. Durant thought fit to submit the following as the report of the Committee:

"GENTLEMEN: — To our memorial asking a general registration of loyal citizens Governor Wells has deemed best to reply only by a publication in the journals.

Without adverting to some errors of fact into which the Governor has fallen on irrelevant questions in regard to former expressions of one of the members of this Committee, it may be said of the Governor's reply that he admits all that we have based our application upon, *i.e.* his right to set aside the provisions of the Constitution of 1864, when necessity required it, which leaves the whole question of government to his own will. He does not, however, consider the extension of the suffrage a case of necessity, requiring his interference, and therefore refuses the prayer of our memorial."

After reading the above, Mr. Durant said that the respectful request of the Central Committee having been refused, it will be well to put the whole matter before the President of the United States. He then read a memorial as follows:

New Orleans, July 13th, 1865.

TO HIS EXCELLENCY, ANDREW JOHNSON,
PRESIDENT OF THE UNITED STATES
Washington City, D.C.

RESPECTED SIR:

The apparent state government in Louisiana, exists solely, by the sufferance of the military authority of the United States.

Its senators and representatives obtained no admission to the Hall of Congress.

Its Governor appeals to the President of the United States, as the fountain of his power.

Shortly after the return of his Excellency Governor Wells, from his recent visit to Washington, the Picayune, newspaper of this city, esteemed his official organ, in an article of the 14th of June, said "Doubts have been expressed in high quarters, in the Congress of the United States and elsewhere, as to the constitutionality and regularity of the existing State Government. The President has guarded against all such doubts by reorganizing and designating Governor Wells as Military Governor."

The power of Governor Wells, no longer rest upon his election, by the small number of legal votes cast for the government which senators Sumner and Wade declared in Congress to be a bogus concern but upon the appointment of the President.

His authority is as lawful, valid and unquestionable as that of General Banks and General Shepley, or as that of Governor Holden of North Carolina.

The truth of these emphatic declarations have never been denied in any quarters. They are conclusive as to the power of Gov. Wells — to comply with the prayer of the memorial lately presented to him, by those who now have the honor to address you.

We ask, in the most respectful manner your attention to the memorial of this Committee to Gov. Wells, and his reply, copies of which are herewith inclosed, and which were published by the Governor, without the formality of conveying to us a written reply.

We now appeal, from the President's Officer, to the President himself, and respectfully pray, that if you should determine to exert any interference in Louisiana affairs in advance of the action of Congress, that you will make it in the path indicated in this memorial.

We have the honor to be, with great respect,

Your obedient Servants.

Signed by the President, T. J. DURANT,

And all the members present.

On motion, the report was received and accepted; and the Corresponding Secretary was instructed to forward the documents to the President of the United States.

The Recording Secretary read the following Ordinance of the Opelousas Police Board, conceived in the most reactionary spirit:

ORDINANCE
Relative to the Police of recently Emancipated Negroes or Freedmen, within the corporate limits of the Town of Opelousas.

Whereas the relations formerly subsisting between master and slave have become changed by the action of the controlling authorities; and whereas it is necessary to provide for the proper police and government of the recently emancipated negroes or freedmen, in their new relations to the municipal authorities;

Sect. 1. Be it therefore ordained by the Board of Police of the Town of Opelousas: That no negro or freedman shall be allowed to come within the limits of the Town of Opelousas, without special permission from his employer, specifying the object of his visit, and the time necessary for the accomplishment of the same. Whoever shall violate this provision, shall suffer imprisonment and two days work on the public streets, or shall pay a fine of two dollars and fifty cents.

Sect. 2. Be it further ordained that every negro or freedman who shall be found on the streets of Opelousas after 10 o'clock at night, without a written pass or permit from his employer, shall be imprisoned and compelled to work five days on the public streets, or pay a fine of five dollars.

Sect. 3. No negro or freedman shall be permitted to rent or keep a house within the limits of the town under any circumstances, and any one thus offending, shall be ejected and compelled to find an employer, or leave the town within twenty-four hours. The lessor or furnisher of the house leased or kept as above, shall pay a fine of ten dollars for each offense.

Sect. 4 No negro or freedman shall reside within the limits of the Town of Opelousas, who is not in the regular service of some white person or former owner, who shall be held responsible for the conduct of said freedman. But said employer or former owner may permit said freedman to hire his time, by special permission in writing, which permission shall net extend over twenty-four hours at any one time. Any one violating the provisions of this section, shall be imprisoned and forced to work for two days on the public streets.

Sect. 5. No public meetings or congregations of negroes or freedmen shall be allowed within the limits of the Town of Opelousas, under any circumstances or for any purpose, without the permission of the Mayor or President of the Board. This prohibition is not intended, however, to prevent freedmen from attending the usual Church services conducted by established ministers of religion. Every freedmen violating this law shall be imprisoned and made to work five days on the public streets.

Sect. 6. No negro or freedman shall be permitted to preach, exhort or otherwise declaim, to congregations of colored people, without a special permission from the Mayor or President of the Board of Police, under the penalty of a fine of ten dollars or twenty days work on the public streets.

Sect. 7. No freedman, who is not in the military service, shall be allowed to carry fire-arms or any kind of weapons, within the limits of the Town of Opelousas without the special permission of his employer, in writing, and approved by the Mayor or President of the Board of Police. Any one thus offending shall forfeit his weapons and shall be imprisoned and made to work five days on the public streets, or pay a fine of five dollars in lieu of said work.

Sect 8. No freedman shall sell, barter or exchange any articles of merchandise of traffic, within the limits of Opelousas, without permission in writing from his employer or the Mayor or President of the Board, under the penalty of the forfeiture of said articles, and imprisonment and one day's labor, or a fine of one dollar in lieu of said work.

Sect. 9. Any freedman found drunk within the limits of the town shall be imprisoned and made to labor five days on the public streets, or pay five dollars in lieu of said labor.

Sect. 10. Any freedman not residing in Opelousas, who shall be found within its corporate limits after the hour of 3 o'clock P.M. on Sunday, without a special written permission from his employer or the Mayor, shall be arrested and imprisoned and made to work two days on the public streets, or pay two dollars in lieu of said work.

Sect. 11. All the foregoing provisions apply to freed men and freed women, or both sexes.

Sect. 12. It shall be the special duty of the Mayor or President of the Board, to see that all the provisions of this ordinance are faithfully executed.

Sect. 13. Be it further ordained, That this ordinance is to take effect from and after its first publication.

Ordained the 3rd day of July, 1865.

E. D. ESTILLETTE,

Jos. D. Richard, Clerk.   President of the Board of Police

July 20, 1865

Mr. Crane, of the Committee on Elections and Vacancies, nominated Mr. J. L. Montieu as Recording Secretary, Capt. Henry Rey as Assistant Recording Secretary and Mr. Wm. Mulford Assistant Corresponding Secretary, who were unanimously elected.

Mr. Crane read a partial report from the Committee on Registration. The plan submitted is substantially this:

1. The Central Executive Committee will act as a Central Board of Registration and Election.

2. Books and a set of instructions will be prepared for the registration of voters in the twenty-three precincts of this city.

3. The rules followed in the registration will be the existing laws and ordinances, except the qualification of "white."

4. The Central Executive Committee will designate three Commissioners and two Clerks in each of the precincts, to act — after being duly sworn — as Registers and Commissioners of Election.

5. All returns will be made to the President of the Central Executive Committee.

6. A place to serve as headquarters will be designated in each of the eleven wards.

7. All questions arising from this matter will be decided in conformity with the instructions of the Corresponding Secretary.

8. The Central Executive Committee will appoint the time to begin operations.

9. This time will be as soon as the Precinct Committee will be organized.

10. Same operations will be conducted in the parishes by friendly persons, and, with the assistance of the Board of Industry and, if possible, of the Bureau of Freedmen.

On motion of Mr. Rufus Waples, the report was referred to the same Committee, to be completed.

Mr. Crane reported a set of regulations for voluntary registration, as follows:

1. Three Commissioners and two Clerks will have charge in each precinct of this city for the voluntary registration, to begin on the second Monday of August next.

2. A similar bureau will be established in each of the country parishes, and the same duty entrusted to them.

3. The registration will embrace all loyal male citizens, native born or naturalized, above twenty-one years of age.

4. The books will contain the name of every registered person, with a full description of said person.

5. Certificates of Registration will be delivered, with a copy of the description.

6. After the registration is completed the books will be sealed up and addressed to the Secretary of the Executive Committee.

A resolution was offered upon a suggestion of Judge Warmoth: That a committee of three be appointed to recommend suitable persons for Commissioners and Clerks.

Messrs. Dunn, Crane and Lynne were appointed committee.

The Recording Secretary was instructed to have the books and blank forms prepared for the work of registration.

August 3, 1865

Mr. Crane submitted — to be considered at the next meeting — several preambles and resolutions, which were ordered to be printed in the *Tribune*.

He explained the main object of these resolutions. They state in substance that:

1. The friends of Universal Suffrage in the several parishes of the State will elect delegates to a State Nominating Convention, to assemble in New Orleans on the 25th of September, with the object of nominating candidates for State offices and consolidating the Universal Suffrage Party.

2. It is recommended that one-half of those delegates be white, and one-half colored.

3. The election for delegates will be held in New Orleans on the 16th of September. The Orleans parish will send six delegates for each representative district, and six for Algiers.

4. Each country parish will similarly send six delegates.

5. The votes in the convention will be counted *per capita*, except for the nominations.

Mr. Crane explained, in a forcible manner, the importance of these resolutions. The Convention will be remarkable for the talented and good men of whom it will be composed. There will be men fully capable of writing the history of the mal-administration of Gov. Wells, and of the murders and assassinations committed upon loyalists. Such a Convention will be of great weight before Congress.

August 10, 1865.

The resolutions of Mr. Crane on the holding of a Convention were taken up. Mr. Crane proposed various amendments, which were all adopted. The election for delegates will be held on the 16th of September next; the poll will be open, in New Orleans, at No. 49 Union street, from 9 o'clock A.M. to 8½ P.M.; the tellers will be appointed in the city by the Central Committee; in the parishes, by the people themselves.

August 31, 1865.

Mr. Durant stated that he wished to submit to the Committee a short circular, for the object of notifying our friends in the State and at the North of the existence of the Central Executive Committee.

The circular was read and adopted:

ROOM OF THE CENTRAL EXECUTIVE COMMITTEE
FRIENDS OF UNIVERSAL SUFFRAGE.

New Orleans, September, 1865.

To:

SIR: — By the terms of a resolution adopted on the evening of 31st August, I have been instructed to send you the names of the officers and members of our Committee, for the purpose of making known to you the existence of an organization to promote the extension of suffrage to all loyal citizens, without distinction of race, and to solicit your aid and assistance.

Very respectfully,

Your obedient servant,

THOMAS J. DURANT.

WM. MULFORD, *Assistant Corresponding Secretary.*   *President.*

OFFICERS OF THE CENTRAL EXECUTIVE COMMITTEE OF THE FRIENDS OF UNIVERSAL SUFFRAGE.

PRESIDENT	THOMAS J. DURANT,
VICE-PRESIDENT	ANTHONY FERNANDEZ,
RECORDING SECRETARY	J. L. MONTIEU,
TREASURER	W. R. CRANE,
CORRESPONDING SECRETARY	H. C. WARMOTH,
ASS'T RECORDING SECRETARY	H. REY,
ASS'T CORRESPONDING SECRETARY	WM. MULFORD

MEMBERS OF THE COMMITTEE.

1. Ansel Edwards,
2. Charles Ogilvie,
3. B. F. Flanders,
4. Henry Train,
5. S. Seiler,
6. A. Commagere,
7. O. J. Dunn,
8. H. Stiles,
9. J. L. Imlay,
10. R. Aberton,
11. C. F. Christophe,
12. Rufus Waples,
13. Thomas Lynne,
14. D. C. Woodruff,
15. Alfred Jervis,
16. Wm. Mulford,
17. E. Warren,
18. Dr. J. White,
19. T. W. Conway.

September 7, 1865.

Mr. Crane offered a set of resolutions, in substance:

1. The parishes are advised to proceed to a registration of loyal disfranchised citizens who have lived in the State for one year, and in the parish for six months.

2. In case that no registration be practicable, clubs will be formed and poll books will be kept at the voluntary election.

3. Votes will be cast for only the officers designated by the Convention.

4. Registration books or poll books, or both, as required, will be furnished to the parishes by the Recording Secretary.

5. Those resolutions will be printed in the *Tribune* and sent to the parishes by the Corresponding Secretary.

Mr. Crane showed how desirable it is that the work of registration be extended to the parishes. An effort should be made to give as much weight and authenticity as possible to our voluntary election. The effect upon Congress will depend upon the mass that we may be able to call to the polls. Registration should be proceeded with everywhere. But if the time is too short, the election itself will constitute a kind of registration.

September 14, 1865.

The St. Lewis de Gonzague Society addressed a contribution of $5. This act is very meritorious, as this Society is composed of aged women, with very limited means.

Mr. Durant presented from some friends of the cause, who do not wish to have their names made public, a contribution of $642 60. [Applause.]

The Secretary read a communication of Mr. François, of Baton Rouge, apprising the Committee that six delegates to the Convention were elected on Saturday, 9th inst., for the parish of Baton Rouge.

The special committee appointed to nominate delegates for the Parish of Orleans, reported a list of names, which, as follows, were unanimously adopted, viz:

Delegates to the Convention of Universal Suffrage.

1st District.

C. Hughes,
W. H. Hire,
W. H. Pearne,

A. W. Lewis,
F. Miles,
W. R. Crane,

2nd District.

Ansel Edwards,
Blanc Joubert,
A. Jervis,

T. W. Conway,
Dr. R.I. Cromwell,
Wm. Mulford.

3rd District.

T.J. Durant,
T. Lynne,
H. C. Warmoth,

P. Bonseigneur,
R. H. Isabelle,
J.A. Craig.

4th District.

S. Seiler,
O.J. Dunn,
R. McCary,

B. Saulay,
C. Dalloz,
Chas. Smith.

5th District.

Aristide Marie,
H. Train,
T. Delassize,

P. Guigonet,
H. B. Ternot,
J. R. Clay.

6th District.

B.F. Flanders,
Bernard Soulié,
A. Fernandez,

A. Commagère,
C. Courcelles,
Laurent Auguste.

7th District.

J. L. Imlay,
R. Aberton,
E. Rillieux,

Armand Lanussé,
Dr. J. White,
Chas. Martinez.

8th District.

Auguste Simon,	Joseph Soudé,
Pierre Cannel,	H. Stiles,
Joseph Curiel,	T. Duvert.

9th District.

E. Warren,	F. C. Christophe,
J.C. Thomas,	Eug. Chessé,
A. Shelly,	Ls. Banks.

10th District.

J.B. Noble,	W.C. Johnson,
Rufus Waples,	Z. Getchell,
D.C. Woodruff,	G. Littlejohn.

11th District, (Algiers.)

Seth Lewis,	Wm. Voss,
E.H. Heath,	L. Boguille,
E. Morphy,	Victor Derinsbourg.

The following is the official report of the Commissioners of Election:

"We certify that at an election held at No. 49 Union street on the 16th day of September, 1865, pursuant to the order of the Central Executive Committee, for 66 delegates, to represent the Parish of Orleans in the Convention of the Friends of Universal Suffrage, to assemble in New Orleans on the 25th inst., the regular ticket, as follows, was duly elected delegates to said Convention:

1st *District* — W.R. Crane, W.H. Hire, C. Hughes, A.W. Lewis, F. Miles, W.H. Pearne.

2nd *District* — T.W. Conway, Dr. R.I. Cromwell, Ansel Edwards, Alfred Jervis, Blanc Joubert, Wm. Mulford.

3rd *District* — P. Bonselgneur, J.A. Craig, T.J. Durant, R.H. Isabelle, T. Lynne, H.C. Warmoth.

4th *District* — O.J. Dunn, C. Dalloz, R. McCary, B. Saulay, S. Seiler, Chas. Smith.

5th *District* — J.R. Clay, T. Delassize, P. Guigonet, Aristidé Marie, J.B. Ternot, H. Train

6th *District* — Laurent Auguste, A. Commagère, O. Courcelles, A. Fernandez, B.F. Flanders, Bernard Soulié.

7th *District* —R. Aberton, J.L. Imlay, Armand Lanussé, Chas. Martinez, E. Rilieux, Dr. J. White.

8th *District* — Pierre Cannel, Joseph Curiel, T. Duvert, Auguste Simon, Joseph Soudé, H. Stiles.

9th *District* — Les. Banks, Eug. Chessé, F.C. Christophe, A. Shelly, J.C. Thomas, E. Warren

10th *District* — Z. Getchell, W.C. Johnson, G. Littlejohn, J.B. Noble, Rufus Waples, D.C. Woodruff.

11th *District* (Algiers) — L. Boguille, Victor Derinsbourg, E.H. Heath, Seth Lewis, E. Morphy, Wm. Voss.

"We further certify that the aggregate vote polled amounts to 2621; and all voters have agreed that a majority of delegates elected shall fill all vacancies in the delegation."

W.R. CRANE, President.
J. L. MONTIEU, Secretary.

J. L. IMLAY, Commissioner,
O. J. DUNN, Commissioner,
R. ABERTON, Commissioner.

Mr. Dunn, from the Committee on Registration, reported progress, and proposed the organization of a Bureau of Registration for Algiers. This matter was referred to the special committee that organized the registration in the Parish of Jefferson.

Mr. A. Jervis submitted important resolutions, in substance as follows:

That the Central Executive Committee suggest a Convention of the Friends of Universal Suffrage in the whole United States, to be held at Philadelphia.

September 28, 1865.

On motion of Mr. Dunn, the propriety of printing a condensed record of the proceedings of the Central Executive Committee, as an introduction to the proceedings of the late Convention, was referred to the Committee on Printing.

PROCEEDINGS OF THE CONVENTION.

MORNING SESSION.

Monday, September, 27, 1865.

The delegates met at twelve o'clock M., at No. 49 Union street. The attendance was very full. The assembly having been called to order by Mr. Crane, Mr. A. Fernandez was chosen President *pro tem.*, and Mr. Montieu. Secretary *pro tem.*

A Committee on Credentials was appointed. Messrs. Train, Delassize and Le. Thomas, (of Baton Rouge,) committee.

On motion of Mr. Train, amended by Mr. Soulié the Convention will hold its next meeting at Economy Hall, at 6 o'clock P.M.

On motion of Mr. Dunn, a committee of five was appointed to report on a permanent organization. Messrs. Dunn, Bonguille, Joubert, Ls. Thomas and Dr. Hire, committee.

The Convention then adjourned.

EVENING SESSION.

The evening session was called to order by Mr. A. Fernandez, and opened by an eloquent prayer by Rev. W.R. Pearne.

Mr. Train then reported from the Committee on Credentials. The names, [see proceedings of Exec. Com., Sept. 18th] already known to our readers, were reported for the Parish of Orleans.

The following names were then reported:

Ascension — Wm. Beaufort, Fred. Fobb, D. Miller. P. F. Valfroit.

Assumption — Peter Hills, G. Nicot, Jas. Johnson, Isaac Richardson, Henry Woodruff, Keynion, Jos. Dupaty, Jean Rotgé, Vincent F. Pintado; Eudaldo G. Pintado.

Baton Rouge — Ls. Thomas, Thomas Murray, Houston Reedy, N. Whiting, A.G. Rogers, Dr. Roberts.

East Feliciana — Tony Steward, A. Marshal, Martin Schnurr.

Iberville —George Deslonde.

Jefferson —Jas Mushaway, Wm. H. Nelson, John Page, Ursin Lavigne, J.H.A. Roberts, Joseph Boutte.

Lafourche — Paul Getridge, Joseph Laney, Henry A. Gallup, R.K. Diossy.

St. Charles —Peter S. Kramer, Thomas Jones, George Gane, Isaac Esaro, John B. Hasly, Thomas Caston.

Terrebonne —R. W. Bennie, A. Rougelot, A. Delage, M. Vance, Grandison Hunter, James Dyer.

All of whom were admitted.

The roll being called, 84 members, of a total of 111, answered to their names.

Mr. Rufus Waples called for the report of the Committee on the Permanent Organization of the Convention.

The report was read. It proposed the name of the Hon. Thomas J. Durant for President of the Convention, which was greeted with great applause as also were those of the following gentlemen: — For Vice-Presidents, B.F. Flanders, A. Fernandez, B. Soulié, R.I. Cromwell and Peter J. Kramer; for Treasurer, W. R. Crane; for Recording Secretary, W. Vigers; Assistant Recording Secretary, J.E. Mathieu; Sergeant-at-Arms, R. C. Baylor; Assistant, Moses Townsend. All of whom were adopted unanimously. A committee of the members being appointed to escort Mr. Durant to the chair, the honorable gentlemen crossed the hall amidst enthusiastic cheering applause.

Mr. Durant thanked the Convention for the unasked honor bestowed upon him. He said that there was but one object to pursue: That is for the welfare of this country and the happiness of humanity at large.

It is obvious to all reflecting minds that after the mighty revolution which plunged this country into war, there was but one remedy which could heal the country's wounds: It was universal liberty, and universal suffrage. [Cheers.]

If liberty is not a mere name, the enfranchised citizen becomes entitled to all the privileges of other citizens. It is true that much latitude must be given to the natural difference of opinions; but in the end, that result must be reached — universal suffrage; and it was to reach that noble end that this Convention was called.

The first steps of this movement, when but a few parishes were represented, were modest ones; but new it reaches to the farthest limits of the State. The honorable gentleman entered after this, into a long explanation of the reasons why the party will have nothing to do with the elections ordered by the Governor by virtue of a constitution whose authority they do not acknowledge, for it was not sanctioned by a majority of the citizens of this State. The only thing left for them to do, is to appeal to the decision of the United States Congress If they carry their project through, they will have given the country a much desired peace which cannot be obtained in any other manner.

On motion of Mr. Dunn, a resolution of thanks to Messrs. A. Fernandez and Montieu for their services, was unanimously adopted.

Mr. Crane moved to appoint a committee of five members, to which will be referred the resolutions to be proposed to the Convention.

The motion was adopted, and the following named gentlemen were appointed: Messrs. Crane, Flanders, Ls. Thomas, of Baton Rouge, and Bennie, of Terrebonne.

Mr. Flanders moved to appoint a committee of five, to draft an address to the people of Louisiana. The motion being adopted, Messrs: Flanders, Soulié, Dunn, Rougelot and Schnurr were appointed on that committee. On motion of Mr. Delage, the name of the President was unanimously added.

It was decided that this committee should report on Tuesday evening.

Mr. Soulié proposed the following resolution:

"It is resolved, that in order to identify this organization with the great Republican party, we now adopt that appellation, and that all acts and resolutions of this Convention be made in the name of the Republican party of Louisiana."

The reading of the resolution opened the door to a long and warm discussion. Dr. Cromwell objected, in an emphatic manner, to its adoption, alleging that the Republican party, as it is organized, might not profess exactly the same principles as those of the political party which it is now proposed to organize in this State.

Mr. Warmoth replied that the National Republican party had committed themselves in favor of universal suffrage; and in proof of this, he alluded to several well-known political men of the North who had emphatically declared themselves in favor of the very reform the Convention wishes now to carry.

Mr. A. Jervis said that no name could better express the aim of the party than the appellation of the "Friends of Universal Suffrage;" but the word republican might leave many in the dark, and the aim of the great party which goes in the North by that name is not so well understood by all.

Mr. Warren spoke at some length in favor of the resolution, saying that in order to give a necessary strength to the party, it would be good policy to merge this organization into the great National Republican Party, which was, after all, as well committed ln favor of universal suffrage as any other party.

Mr. Gallup, of Lafourche, proposed to strike out, in the resolution, all that precedes the words "*that all acts.*"

Mr. Crane moved to refer the resolution with the amendment to the Committee on Resolutions. Carried.

On Mr. Train's motion, the Convention adjourned till 6 o'clock to-morrow.

Tuesday Evening, Sept. 26, 1865.

The Convention met at 6 o'clock, pursuant to adjournment. The roll having been called, 62 members answered to their names.

Mr. Vigers, Secretary, read the minutes of the previous meeting, which were approved.

Mr. Crane of the Committee on Resolutions, read their report on sundry resolutions presented the night before to the Convention. The report was received.

Mr. Warmoth asked leave to present a resolution, which was granted.

The resolutions reported by Mr. Crane were then taken up, as follows:

1. *Resolved* — That this body shall be styled the Convention of the Republican Party in Louisiana, and does hereby reaffirm the platform of principles adopted at Baltimore, in June, 1864, by the Convention which nominated Abraham Lincoln and Andrew Johnson.

2. *Resolved* — That the Ordinance of Secession adopted by a Convention of the people of Louisiana, called by an act of the Legislature, was a declaration

25

of war against the United States; it disrupted in fact, though not in law, the relations existing between the General Government and the people of this State and rendered the latter incapable of exercising the privileges of citizens of the United States.

3. *Resolved* — In addition, that the acts of Congress of the United States, declaring the inhabitants of Louisiana to be in a state of insurrection, constituted them, in law, enemies of the United States, and unfitted them for the functions of a State in the Union until restored by the action of Congress.

4. *Resolved* — That loyal *State* Governments are essential to the Government of the United States, without which it cannot operate; that the rebellion was carried on by insurgent *States*, and the object of the war was to subdue these and erect in their places loyal *States*; therefore it is the duty of the United States, at the earliest possible moment consistent with the general welfare, to establish; by act of Congress, a Republican Government in Louisiana.

5. *Resolved* — That this duty is imposed by the Constitution on "the United States," and not on any military commander or Executive officer but must be performed by the United States, represented by the President and both houses of Congress.

6. *Resolved* — That the system of slavery heretofore existing ln Louisiana, and the laws and ordinances passed from time to time to support it, have ceased to exist; and we protest against any and all attempts to substitute in their place a system of serfdom, or forced labor in any shape.

7. *Resolved* — That the necessities of the Nation called the colored men into the public service, in the most honorable of all duties — that of the soldier fighting for the integrity of his country and the security of the Constitutional Government; this, with his loyalty, patience and prudence, are sufficient to assure Congress of the justice and safety of giving him a vote to protect his liberty.

8. *Resolved* — That it would be unwise to admit the inhabitants of Louisiana at once into the Union as a State. A preliminary System of local government should be established by Congress, to endure so long as may be necessary, to test the fidelity of the people to the United States, and to accustom the inhabitants to exercise in harmony and peace the rights and duties of self-government.

9. *Resolved* — That this Convention reaffirms the principles set forth in the Declaration of American Independence in 1776: — That all men were created equal; and that republican and just governments require the consent of the governed; and deem this a fitting occasion to repeat and reaffirm our convictions in these great truths from the peculiar circumstances in which our loyal fellow-citizens of African descent are placed — though equal in numbers to the white race; denied all political rights, and governed without their consent; subjected to taxation without representation, and subjected to trials by courts and juries, and denied all participation in their organization and administration.

10. *Resolved* — That this Convention adopts, as the basis of its political organization, universal suffrage, liberty and the equality of all men before the law.

11. *Resolved* — That under existing circumstances, this Convention considers it inexpedient to nominate candidates for State officers.

12. *Resolved* — That this Convention respectfully recommends to the Republican party of the United States. and all friends of equal laws and equal rights, the propriety of holding, at an early day, a National Convention, organized on the basis of this Convention, one-half white and the other half colored, to adopt a national platform on the basis of universal suffrage, and to consider the questions suggested by the foregoing resolutions.

Mr. Train proposed, as an amendment, to strike out, in the first resolution, the words *Republican Party*, and substitute the words "the Loyal Universal Suffrage Party." He objected to being merged into the Republican party, whose policy is not settled yet.

Mr. Conway and Dr. Lewis defended the Republican party, and briefly reviewed its history.

Mr. Jervis and Capt. Isabelle showed that the republican party has not been, up to this time, in favor of universal suffrage.

Mr. Charles Smith wanted to have no misunderstanding and to go frankly for universal suffrage.

Mr. Gallup made a lengthy defense of the Republican party. He said that from its first day that party was opposed to slavery in the territories; and as the rebel States are now considered in the light of territories, that plank of the earliest Republican platform covers, at this present moment, the case of the Southern States as well as it did in 1856 Kansas and the Western Territories.

The amendment being put to the vote, was declared lost; 41 nays against yeas.

The first resolution was then adopted as originally proposed by the committee: The other resolutions, down to No. 9, were severally read and adopted, *nem. con.*

Mr. Gallup proposed, as an amendment to the 9th resolution, to strike out the words "our loyal fellow-citizens of African descent," and insert the words "one-half of our fellow-citizens." The amendment was laid on the table, and the resolution, as reported by the committee, was adopted.

The 10th and 11th resolutions were adopted unanimously.

Mr. Gallup moved to amend the 12th resolution by striking out the words "on the basis of this Convention, one-half white and one-half colored," and insert the words, "without distinction of race or color." Adopted.

Resolutions were offered by Mr. Warmoth, and adopted, endorsing measures of the General Government in suppressing the rebellion.

Adjourned, to 7 o'clock to-morrow evening.

Wednesday Evening, September 27, 1865.

The Convention was called to order at 6 o'clock P.M., Hon. T.J. Durant in the chair.

The roll being called, 54 members answered to their names.

Mr. Vigers, Secretary, read the minutes of the previous meeting, which were approved.

On motion of Mr. Dunn, Chaplain Conway opened the proceedings with a soul stirring prayer.

The Committee on Credentials reported certain members who presented themselves for the first time this evening.

These delegates are:

Parish of St. Mary — Messrs. Arthur Antoine, C.P. Bouté, Pierre Romain, Louis Nicholas, E. Rassmiss Hunt, Hely Barry.

The order of the day was the report of the Committee on Address. Mr. Flanders, chairman of that Committee, read the address prepared by them. The address was received and adopted unanimously, as follows:

ADDRESS OF THE STATE REPUBLICAN CONVENTION TO THE PEOPLE OF LOUISIANA.

The Convention of the Republican party deem it impolite to make nominations for State officers at the present time. We have not had the means of communication through the State necessary to such a complete interchange of ideas as would be required for this result.

The entire civil and political constitution of Louisiana has been changed by the rebellion. The insurgent State authorities claimed independence and the perpetuation of slavery. They have been expelled from the State; and slavery, with all the laws, ordinances and regulations to which it gave rise, has been swept away by the tempest of war.

The people of African descent are now free and as free as all other men. This truth must be recognized and carried out in all its legitimate consequences. The best minds in the South, as well as in the North, do not hesitate to adopt it.

Hamilton, Provisional Governor of Texas, declared by special proclamation, that colored men must be placed, in Texas, on an absolute equality with white men, in all trials for crimes and offences.

Marvin, Provisional Governor of Florida, says to the people there, "By the operations and results of the war, slavery has ceased to exist in this State. It cannot be revived. Every voter for delegates to the Convention, in taking the amnesty oath, takes a solemn oath to support the freedom of the former slave. The freedom intended is the full, ample and complete freedom of a citizen of the United States. This does not necessarily include the privilege of voting, but it does include the idea of full constitutional guarantees of future possession and quiet enjoyment. The question of his voting is an open question — a proper subject for discussion — and is to be decided as a question of sound policy by the convention to be called."

Parsons, Provisional Governor of Alabama, declared: "Now that slavery is dead, I can conceive no greater social evil than a class of humanity in our midst so excluded from the civil pale as to become a stagnant, seething, miasmatic, moral cesspool in the community. Human nature either improves or degenerates — it cannot stand still; but it cannot improve without the moral incentive of hope and a human future. Therefore the freedman must, for our own security as well as his, be brought at once within the pale of civil law. His citizenship must be recognized. As a man, without any reference to his discretion or social position, he is entitled to life, liberty and the pursuit of happiness. With this view I have welcomed the chivalrous proposition of Gen. Swayne, and have advised my appointees, in good faith, to admit the freedman to the courts."

Nor can these truths and their consequences be denied. Every free man, a native of the United States, or naturalized, is a citizen according to the highest legal authorities. Every emancipated slave, therefore, has obtained with his freedom the title of a citizen of the United States. Such is the inevitable consequence of freedom.

In the election which has been ordered by Gov. Wells, every voter must swear, in the presence of his God, that he will support the abolition of slavery. Here is the oath which he must take. It is the condition of amnesty allowed him by President Johnson:

"I do solemnly swear or affirm, in the presence of Almighty God, that I will henceforth faithfully defend the Constitution of the United States, and the union of States thereunder, and *that I will in like manner abide by, and faithfully support, all laws and proclamation which have been made during the existing rebellion, with reference to the emancipation of slaves.*"

There is no reservation. Every voter is bound, in conscience and in honor, to treat every man, white or black, as free; and to treat him as he would wish himself to be treated.

But can we "faithfully support" the freedom of the colored man if we withhold from him the means of supporting it himself?

The citizenship of the entire population is not a novel idea in Louisiana. The third article of the treaty of Paris, by which Louisiana was ceded to the United States in 1803, provided: "That the inhabitants of the ceded territory shall be incorporated in the Union of the United States and admitted as soon as possible, according to the principles of the Federal Constitution, to the enjoyment of all the rights, advantages and immunities of citizens of the United States."

The repressive influence of slaves prevented the full application of this article; but slavery is now no more. The treaty is the supreme law of the land; and the rights of guarantees are imprescriptible.

A few years after this treaty was made, one who never spoke anything he did not mean, expressly called the free colored men of Louisiana, "fellow-citizens," when he invited them to arm to repel the invasion of the State.

The code of Louisiana admitted, even under the system of slavery, the free men of color to testify for or against parties, without regard to origin, in all cases, civil or criminal, in our courts; and almost every trade and pursuit was open to him, at least as far as the legal theory was concerned, however limited by prejudice.

We submit to the understandings of our fellow-citizens, that in no case has the State suffered by this concession; and that whether as a soldier or a citizen, the free man of color has invariably shown himself, in all the ennobling qualities of man, the equal of his more favored fellow-citizen, nor has he ever ceased to be a useful member of the State, when treated with justice and equity; and that what those formerly free have been, the newly emancipated class is prepared to be.

The people of African descent are not to be held responsible for the present condition of affairs. They deserve no man's anger for the situation. They did not organize the rebellion. They did not carry on the war. Both the belligerents invoked their assistance, which was afforded freely to those who assured their liberty.

Do not continue in the delusion that "a few fanatics in the North and South" produced the great rebellion and its grand results. Philosophy turns with disdain from the reasoning which would impute such immense consequences to causes of so trifling a nature. In our country ideas are omnipotent. The idea of slavery was incompatible with that of liberty. They could not continue to exist together; and slavery was too arrogant to yield peacefully to its inevitable fate. The idea to which it gave place, and before which it fell, should be fully carried out in the new system of government to be inaugurated.

Louisiana has not yet been recognized as a State readmitted into the Union. Senators and representatives, setting up claims to seats in Congress, have not gained admittance.

The Constitution of 1864 was adopted by a fragment only of the people of the State; and the registration which even that fragment effected in the city of New Orleans, which cast by far the larger portion of the vote has been repudiated and annulled by the Governor himself.

The provisions of the Constitution of 1864 have never been observed by the Executive, unless where they were conformable to his own will. There has been no State Government here, save that which the Governor, tempted by the military authorities, saw fit to give us. This fact, coupled with the grave defects which existed in the authority which called the Convention that framed the Constitution, and in the election and conduct of that body, is sufficient to set aside the theory that any State Government, legally speaking, now exists in Louisiana; the organization partially performing the functions of such, being merely an adjunct of the military power of the United States.

Under these circumstances it seems proper that a delegate should be chosen to present the views and feelings of the republicans of Louisiana at Washington during the coming session of Congress. In the wisdom and patriotism of that body we place our reliance, and look with confidence to its action, to solve in the spirit of justice and humanity the great question of Reconstruction.

Mr. Warmoth presented the following resolution:

Resolved — That this Convention do now proceed to the formation of a constitution, to be submitted to the people for their ratification *or* rejection, at the next election, preparatory to the admission of Louisiana into the Union as a State.

In support of his resolutions, Mr. Warmoth remarked that if it was pronounced exceptionable, it was to be borne in mind that Louisiana was in an exceptionable condition; for since New Orleans was taken by the federal forces, it may be properly said that Louisiana was no State; but it is governed by military rule, the will of one man. The Constitution of 1852 has lost all its authority; and the other one of 1864 was never ratified by a majority of the people, nor was it sanctioned by the Federal Government. It was unnecessary to frame a new constitution; it would be but necessary to strike out from that of 1864 a few words by which most of the loyal people of Louisiana are excluded from the polls, and will be so forever, if no remedy be resorted to immediately.

During the latter portion of his eloquent speech, Mr. Warmoth was interrupted every now and then, by the most enthusiastic applause; and when he sat down, it was amidst stamping of feet, clapping of hands and lusty cheers.

Capt. Isabelle made a learned defense of Mr. Warmoth's resolution.

Mr. Conway moved to make that resolution the order of the day for tomorrow. Adopted. The same gentleman then read the following, which was unanimously adopted:

Resolved — That this Convention do hereby adopt the New Orleans Tribune as the official organ of the Republican party of the State of Louisiana, and that all friends of Republican Government are advised and encouraged to give to that organ their fullest and most cordial support and patronage.

Mr. Craig offered a resolution to the effect that this Convention nominate a delegate to Congress, to represent the Territory in the National Councils, preparatory to its reorganization as a State of the Union.

The consideration of the resolution was postponed to the next meeting.

The Convention adjourned till 10 o'clock A.M.

Thursday, September 28, 1865.

The Convention assembled at 10 o'clock, pursuant to adjournment.

The Rev. R. McCary opened the proceedings with an eloquent prayer. The Secretary then read the minutes of the previous meeting, which were adopted.

The order of the day was Mr. Warmoth's resolution proposing to the Convention to prepare a Constitution, to be submitted to the people for rejection or adoption.

Mr. Rufus Waples opposed the resolution. In his opinion it was injudicious at this time, and inconsistent with the resolutions already unanimously adopted as the sense of this Convention on the subject. We have not been sent here as delegates to form a constitution; but even if we had the power, it would be highly impolitic and almost suicidal to exercise it. What are we to understand by the term *State*? By the law of nations France is a state; Russia is a State; England is not, but the United Kingdom of Great Britain, Scotland and Ireland, is a State. The United States constitute a State. In this sense, Louisiana is not, and never was, a State. The Secessionists erred in treating Louisiana as a State under the law of nations; for, under that law, a State is a nation.

In the constitution of the United States the term "State" has a much more limited signification. Massachusetts is a State, in this sense, but not a nation. Three elements are necessary to constitute a State, under the Federal Constitution:

1st. Citizens owing allegiance to the United States.

2nd. Land

3rd. Constitutional organization not repugnant to the Federal Constitution.

The destruction of any of these three elements must cause the existence of the State to cease. No State can secede from the Union, because no State is a nation; because no State can divest the Federal Government of its jurisdiction, (however unanimous the citizens of the State might be in favor of seceding;) because all the citizens composing the Republic have rights in each State, of which they cannot be divested against their will. But if any one of the essential three elements be wanting, the State ceases, and the land and the citizens remain under the Federal Government only. The first element, land is permanent. It is possible that the second element, loyal citizens, may fail; for all the inhabitants of a new State, upon the Indian frontier, on account of Indian depredations and fears, for their personal safety, might possibly seek older settlements and leave the land of the new State depopulated. It is manifest that, the new State would cease to be such, for want of citizens. The third element, a constitutional organization not repugnant to the Federal Constitution, may easily be destroyed. The citizens of Massachusetts may call a constitutional convention repeal their constitution, and then adjourn *sine die*, without forming another. Being then without any constitutional organization, Massachusetts would cease to be a State for want of one of the essential elements. If, without abolishing their constitution altogether, the citizens of Massachusetts should make it repugnant to the Federal Constitution the third element would still be wanting, and Massachusetts would cease to be a State.

Louisiana ceased to be a State from the moment her constitutional organization became repugnant to the Federal Constitution; that is, she ceased to be a *State* in the constitutional sense of that term. Although the Ordinance of Secession was an absolute nullity, the striking out of the words "United States" from the Constitution, and inserting "Confederate States," and the requiring of officers to swear allegiance to the latter instead of the former, made the whole instrument repugnant to the Federal Constitution. From that moment Louisiana ceased to have such a constitution as the Constitution of the United States requires each State to have (admitting, for argument sake, that she had such a constitution before.) She therefore ceased to be a State. The land remained and the citizens remained — both under the exclusive control of the Federal Government.

But although the citizens remained on the land, they did not remain *loyal* citizens, maintaining their allegiance to the United States. They were not such citizens as the Federal Constitution requires. The changing of their constitution, making it repugnant as above shown, destroyed two essential elements, and nothing was left but the land. The inhabitants not only destroyed their *status* as loyal citizens of the United States, but they became insurrectionists and took up arms against the General Government. This is not such a *State-citizenship* as the Federal Constitution requires. Louisiana ceased to be in harmony with the Federal Government and became antagonistic to it.

Mr. Waples next proceeded to show that the legislative, executive and judicial departments of the Government have all acted in consonance with this theory. In the act of July 13th, 1861, the inhabitants of Louisiana and other rebel States are declared to be in a state of insurrection. By the act of May 20th, 1862, they are designated "insurgents." By the act of March 3rd, 1863, a distinction is drawn between *loyal* States and *disloyal* States. By an act of August 5th, 1861, they are styled States in actual rebellion. By an act of July 17th, 1862, a distinction is recognized between "loyal States" and the "so-called Confederate States of America." An act of July 2nd, 1864, is entitled "an act in addition to the several acts concerning commercial intercourse between *loyal* and *insurrectionary States*," etc. There are many other acts of like import, continuing through the latest legislation of Congress. The President approved all these acts; and has also, in various proclamations and messages, used the same terms, and has treated these insurrectionary districts as parts of the country which had forfeited their State privileges. He says that loyal State governments have been subverted; he speaks of re-establishing a State government which shall be Republican; of constructing a loyal State government; of setting up a State government; of reinaugurating loyal State governments; of reviving a State government, etc., etc.; expressions which are in perfect harmony with the theory that Louisiana and other insurrectionary districts have been destroyed as States, and in perfect discord with the opposite theory.

The Supreme Court has made a distinction between the United States and the so-called Confederate States; they say "the present civil war between the United States and the so-called Confederate States has such character and magnitude as to give the United States the same rights and powers which they might exercise in case of a national and foreign war; that "all persons residing within the *hostile territory*, whose property may be said to increase the resources of the hostile power, are, in this contest, liable to be treated as enemies," etc.

In 2d Black, p. 673, the Supreme Court, speaking of the insurgents, said: "In organizing this rebellion they have *acted as States* claiming to be sovereign over all powers and property within their respective limits, and asserting a right to absolve their citizens from their allegiance to the Federal Government. Several of these States have combined to form a new confederacy, claiming to be acknowledged by the world as a sovereign State. Their right to do so is now being decided by wager of battle. The ports and territory of each of these States are held in hostility to the Central Government. It is no loose, unorganized insurrection, having no defined boundary or possession. It has a boundary marked by lines of bayonets, and which can be crossed only by force; — south of this line is enemies' territory, because it is claimed and held in possession by an organized, hostile and belligerent power.

Thus every department of the Government — legislative, executive and judicial — has taken the legal view which this Convention has adopted.

This position is not only true in law, but in fact. The rebel districts have not performed their functions as States during the past four years; they did not respond when the President called for 75,000 troops; they did not respond when he, soon after, called for 300,000; they did not respond to any of his subsequent calls; they did not pay their taxes; they did not keep representation in Congress; they failed in all the duties of States. Besides their sins of omission they have sins of commission which cannot be overlooked. They attempted to make treaties with foreign powers; they sent ambassadors abroad; they meddled with postal and revenue affairs; they raised armies, without consent of Congress; they fought against the Government; they formed alliances among themselves; they denied the authority of "the supreme law of the land;" all of which is inconsistent with the idea that they continued actually to be *States* in the constitutional sense of the term.

Mr. Waples next proceeded to show that it is not only legal to treat the insurrectionary districts as such, but highly *expedient*. It is the true policy of the country. The dignity of the Republic requires that the inhabitants of any district declared in insurrection shall be denied State privileges until they shall voluntarily petition for admission into the Union, with a constitution not repugnant to that of the United States. State blessings should not be forced upon them. When they shall fully feel the importance of admission into the Union as States, they will petition for it. In the meantime, the nation can afford to wait. If it should take South Carolina ten years to become educated in Republican principles so as to make her anxious for State privileges, that would be far better than her premature admission into the Union. Ten years is a short period in the life of a great nation. Let us not give either South Carolina or Louisiana occasion to complain of being kept in the Union against her will.

Again, the protection of Southern Unionists requires the adopted of this policy. They are infinitely more safe under Congress than under a State legislature. The loyal voters of Louisiana are a small minority; the rebel voters are vastly in majority. If Louisiana is a State, the Unionists will inevitably be subjected to taunts, persecutions, denial of free speech, and to all the embarrassments under which they labored at the beginning of the war. Under the plea of States rights, the majority will object to any action on the part of the Federal Government for the protection of those of whom that Government claims allegiance, although protection and allegiance are correlative. States have rights — the National Government has rights, too. Property administered, these rights do not conflict. But the Unionists of Louisiana do not believe that the majority of voters here will exercise State rights any better now than heretofore; and they are not willing to exchange their protection by the Federal Government for the vain hope of protection by that majority, in the present state of things. Let matters remain as they are till the spirit of the majority in Louisiana shall have been improved by time.

Again, this policy should be adopted in justice to the loyal citizens heretofore disfranchised. If Louisiana is not a State, all who compose the second necessary element, that is, citizens owing allegiance to the Federal Government would have a right to take part in framing the organic law. "Governments derive their just powers from the consent of the governed." This axiom applies to State Governments as much as to the Federal Government. The black inhabitants of Louisiana are a part of "the governed." They are no longer represented or misrepresented by their masters, so-called. Minors and women are part of the governed, but they are represented by parents, guardians, husbands, etc. It is generally admitted that their exclusion from the polls is based upon their own consent; and therefore the fundamental principle of our Republican system, expressed in the axiom just quoted, is not violated in their case. But the blacks do not consent to be excluded from the polls, nor are they represented by others. They therefore do *now* possess the right, without further legislation, to take part as voters in the formation of a new constitution for Louisiana, with the view to her readmission into the Union as a State. This is not only legal and just, but also expedient and desirable. It places the friends of the country in the majority. It secures Republican government, freedom of speech and personal protection. The loyal colored inhabitants should be allowed to take part in the formation of a State government, and in its subsequent administration:

1. Because it would tend to remove the prejudice existing against them, which is the fruitful source of our national and domestic troubles.

2. Because it would tend to secure peace and promote harmony among all classes.

3. Because it would ensure a majority against treason; and against slavery, the basis of the late rebellion.

4. Because it would encourage our valuable agricultural population (composed almost exclusively of blacks) to remain among us to develop the resources of the State, and prevent the threatened forcible expatriation of the loyal white men.

5. Because it would tend to improve and elevate the blacks, cultivate self-respect and laudable ambition, and thus render them more valuable as citizens.

6. Because they are educated to hate slavery, treason and rebellion, and may therefore be safely trusted with a voice upon the great questions growing out of the war.

7. Because they have been too long unjustly deprived of a privilege which is their inalienable right, under our theory of government.

8. Because giving them the right of suffrage would remove the charge of inconsistency made by foreign statesmen and publicists against our Republic.

9. Because it would increase the whole number of voters, and thus render election frauds and corruptions more difficult.

10. Because the blacks are loyal, and would therefore be valuable to the Federal Government in maintaining its interests here.

The people of Louisiana having been declared in insurrection; the State having been destroyed; the Federal Government remaining the only legal authority having jurisdiction here; the "governed," having the right to make a new State organization, (whether the governed be white or black, or both) it may be asked: "Why then should we not at once proceed to make a new constitution, expressly provide that all male adults may vote, and submit the constitution to the whole people for adoption or rejection?" The answer is, that the present state of the public mind is not favorable to such action, at the present time. The colored people have the right to vote, but they would be disturbed in the exercise of that right. If we had the power now in this Convention to make a Republican constitution, it could not be carried into effect in the country parishes, for the national troops would probably be withdrawn as soon as we should be admitted as a State. Persecution, thuggery and unfair dealing towards the new voters would follow. The wronged would appeal to courts and juries in vain. They would have the legal right to redress for their grievances, but they would be practically denied the legal remedy. The slave has had the legal right to the writ of *habeas corpus* ever since the Constitution of the United States was adopted; for that writ is not confined to whites, nor to citizens, nor to freemen, nor to inhabitants of the country. A. Hottentot, an hour after landing upon our shores, if held in durance, has ever had the right to this writ, by which the validity of his arrest and deprivation of liberty could be examined. And yet four millions of persons have been held in durance, with the legal right to the writ, but without the ability practically to exercise it. The colored man would find his rights, as a voter, trampled upon by disloyal white men, and he would find his legal remedy fail him.

He would be driven to the last resort — and who wants a war of races? None but a madman. On the other hand, if we remain under the exclusive control of the Federal Government in a condition similar to that of the territories till the bitterness engendered by the war shall have been somewhat allayed; until the whites shall have seen the colored citizens are sober, industrious and eminently law-abiding; until their present vague hopes of restoring slavery in another form shall have been dissipated, we may then act with certainty of success. If, while we are waiting, the General Government should adopt the policy of recognizing the insurrectionary districts as States never destroyed and indestructible, (contrary to law and fact) then it might be wise to proceed without further delay in inaugurating a movement of all citizens to form a Republican State government, deriving its powers from the consent of all the governed, notwithstanding the difficulties suggested. Mr. Waples remarked, in conclusion, that the Convention had already unanimously adopted the true theory in the resolutions constituting the Republican platform of Louisiana. You have resolved, further, that it would be unwise to admit the inhabitants of Louisiana at once into the Union as a State. These principles have been held by the true loyalists of Louisiana for the past two or three years. In the "Convention of the Friends of Freedom," held in Lyceum Hall, New Orleans, December 15th, 1863, it was unanimously

"Resolved —That the State governments of the rebellious States were unjustly and illegally disorganized, subverted and overthrown, by the hands of armed traitors; and the subsequent conquest of the territory of those States does not operate the restoration of the State governments.

"Resolved — That the only proper method for the insurrectionary districts to pursue, in order to regain their position as States in the Union is to call conventions, adopt constitutions for the new States and petition Congress for admission into the Union.

"Resolved — That so far from objecting to the organization of territorial governments for the States subverted by the rebels, we consider such organization the safest course and the surest method to secure free State governments; the most effectual remedy for the evils of recession; the plan

most likely to satisfy the malcontents, as they would be debarred the plea of being kept in the Union against their will."

Mr. Waples avowed himself the author of these resolutions, and stated that the Hon. B.F. Flanders and Charles W. Honor, Esq., acted with him on the committee which reported them, with other resolutions, to the Convention. They were adopted, at that early day, without a dissenting voice, as before remarked. They contained, even then, no new doctrine, so far as the speaker was concerned. Before a single State had passed its ordinance of secession, he had contended that should any State, or people thereof, disown allegiance to the Federal Government, the latter would have the right to treat such State and people as in a provincial or territorial condition. He was not now giving the Convention the crude and undigested notion of the moment, but the settled conviction of his mind upon the subject.

Our hope is in Congress. We must labor to disabuse the minds of loyal Northern members of the effect of the insidious argument that it would be unjust to Southern loyalists to treat them as the inhabitants of territories. It would be their salvation. The speaker knew that the Northern members had heretofore been much staggered by this argument; and, in their commendable desire to protect the rights of the few in the South who have remained steadfast in their loyalty, they seem to have forgotten that the worst evil that can befall us is the banding of us over to the cruel mercies of our enemies. If this policy should prevail we may all exclaim: "Let our name be Ichabod, for the glory has departed!"

Mr. Crane spoke most earnestly against the resolution. Mr. Conway presented the following amendment:

"*Resolved* — That the subject of the formation of a State Constitution be committed by this Convention to the State Central Committee, and that said Committee be, and is, hereby, empowered to dispose of the subject according to its best judgment."

In defense of this resolution, Mr. Warmoth said that in his opinion it would not be inconsistent nor bad policy for the Republican part to frame a State Constitution. The only objection to it might be that as the Convention represents but a few parishes of the State, the constitution formed by them would lack, as well as that of 1864, the sanction of the majority which alone could invest it with authority. But as to the right of the Convention to propose a constitution, certainly they have it; for any one citizen in a territory has a right to write a constitution and assemble his fellow-citizens and propose to them to approve that document; and if adopted by the majority, it becomes the law of the land. As for the alleged inexpediency of the proposed measure, Mr. Warmoth remarked that if the friends of universal liberty and equally are now opposed to the admission of Louisiana as a State, their only objection is that the constitution of 1864, by which the majority of the white inhabitants pretend to be now ruled, does not grant the colored population their political rights. Let us then frame a constitution which will recognize those rights; for the moment is not far off when it will be absolutely necessary to recognize the State. It will be impossible for the Federal Government to hold the Southern States under one man's power for several years, until the political training of the white man be reformed.

Dr. Cromwell spoke in favor of Mr. Warmoth's resolution, saying that now was the time for the colored man to take this matter in hand and participate in the framing of the constitution which he wishes to live under.

Messrs. Houston Reedy and Jervis spoke against that measure altogether, while Messrs. Curiel and Thomas, of Baton Rouge, declared themselves for the amendment. The latter was finally adopted.

Mr. Soulié presented a resolution in regard to the nomination of two delegates to Congress. Mr. Soulié moved, as an amendment, to strike out the word "two," and substitute the word "one." Mr. Craig would prefer two delegates, one white and the other colored. The latter would have a chance of being invited to take a seat in the House, which would be a great step towards progress; and besides, it is most probable that he could have an interview with the President, and let him know the feelings, the wants, the sufferings and the hopes of the colored population of Louisiana.

Dr. Lewis said a few words in favor of sending but one delegate, while Mr. Noble was, on the contrary, for sending a colored delegate along with the other one. Mr. Blanc Joubert wanted to know where the money for keeping two delegates in Washington, for six or eight months, will come from. It is very well to say that two or four delegates would be better than one, but who are the parties to pay for the expense? It is said that it would be a good stroke to send a colored man to Washington — a clever, decent and gentlemanlike one, an honor to the race — to show the Washington people what are the America born citizens, whom the Southern white people deprive of their political rights. Do those who speak so imagine that the Congressmen, the President and other politicians have not already seen colored men of all degrees, all ranks and hues?

Mr. Flanders said that if we considered Louisiana as a territory, we are not entitled to more than one delegate; and that delegate having to compete with the most experienced gentlemen of the South, must have many qualifications of mind, manners, experience, talents and weighty influence. But it would be well if the other friends of the cause in Louisiana would go along with him to give him additional weight.

Mr. Rufus Waples rose to a point of order. It was decided last night that there would be but one delegate sent to the Capitol, therefore all that discussion is out of order. Agreed to.

Mr. Hire moved that the Convention proceed by ballot to nominate one delegate. Carried. Mr. Durant appointed Messrs. Jean Rotgé, A.W. Lewis, O.J. Dunn and John Page, as tellers. He thanked those members who proposed him for the nomination; but he was compelled to decline that honor for several weighty reasons, the principal one of which is that when the movement of universal suffrage was commenced he resolved to accept of no office, honor or emolument connected with it, in order to be entirely untrammelled with personal interest in the matter. (Applause.)

Mr. Warmoth was nominated by an overwhelming: majority, and the nomination declared unanimous.

On motion of Mr. Soulié, the Convention reconsidered their vote of yesterday, on his resolutions regarding the Central Executive Committee. Agreed to, and the following substituted:

1. *Resolved* — That the present Central Executive Committee of the Friends of Universal Suffrage be continued as the *Central State Executive Committee*, with the addition of five country members, to be chosen by the Committee.

2. That said Committee have charge of all business connected with the objects and wishes of the party and the advancement of its best interests.

3. That said Committee shall sit at least once month at such place in the city and time as they may select, after sufficient notice in the organ of the party and shall have the right to fill all vacancies that may occur in their body.

4. That said Central State Executive Committee be empowered to raise funds by contributions or otherwise, to meet the wants of the party organization, and to disburse the same, provided that no appropriation shall have effect without the concurrence of two-thirds of the members present; and provided, also, that all appropriations exceeding one hundred dollars shall lie over to the next meeting.

5. That a majority of the members returned shall be a quorum to transact business.

Mr. J. A. Craig proposed that the Central Committee have, as soon as practicable, the proceedings of this Convention published in pamphlet form. Carried.

Mr. Joseph S. Soude moved that a vote of thanks be tendered by this Convention to the Economy and Mutual Assistance Society, for the use of the hall for this Convention, and that the President give the necessary instructions to the Secretary to send a letter to the President and members of the Society to that effect. Carried.

Mr. Conway moved that a collection be taken up to defray the expenses of the Convention, and that the same be placed in the hands of the President, to be by him transferred to the Treasurer of the Central Executive Committee for disbursement. Carried. The hat was passed around and the sum of $55 20 was collected.

Mr. Craig moved that the member elected as delegate to Washington be invited to address the Convention at 6 o'clock in the evening. Adopted.

Mr. Jervis proposed that the poll books and ballots cast at the next election for delegates to Congress be returned to the President of the Central Executive Committee of the Republican Party of Louisiana, and he, together with the Secretary, count the same and the President is authorized to furnish credentials to the candidate receiving the highest number of votes. Adopted.

Capt. Noble offered a resolution tendering the thanks of the Convention to the Central Executive Committee, for the services they have rendered the people.

Mr. Warmoth asked to be excused from delivering a speech this evening, and offered reasons, which were accepted.

Mr. Seiler introduced a resolution thanking Mr. Thomas J. Durant for the courteous manner and impartial spirit with which he presided over the meetings of the Convention.

A substitute, offered by Mr. Soudé, including all the officers and committees of the Convention, was adopted unanimously.

Mr. Durant delivered a short but feeling speech, in response to the resolution of thanks just adopted.

Rev. Mr. Conway closed the proceedings with one of those eloquent prayers which spring forth so naturally from his heart to his lips, and the Convention adjourned *sine die*.

November 13, 1865.

The printing of this pamphlet having been delayed, we are enabled to give the result of the election for a delegate to Congress under the auspices of the Central Executive Committee of the Republican party of Louisiana.

The election took place, according to the plan of the Committee and Convention on Monday, the 6th day of November, in the same manner as the elections of the parties claiming to be the only authorized legal electors. Polls were opened by the commissioners of election, and the votes cast for the nominee of the Convention, Judge H.C. Warmoth, according to the official returns received by the Central Executive Committee, were as follows, viz:

Parish of Orleans		9,082
"	" Jefferson	2,669
"	" St. John the Baptist	874
"	" St. Charles	813
"	" Ascension	756
"	" Point Coupee	824
"	" St. Tammany	1,136
"	" Terrebonne	1,358
"	" East Baton Rouge	1,836
"	" West Baton Rouge	492
	Total	18,840

For the want of time, and persons to organize and hold elections in most of the other parishes, no elections took place. It is evident from the facts of the outrages committed, as authentically stated in various communications received by the Executive Committee, that no elections would have been permitted in any of the parishes where the military authority is not paramount. The following cases are in point:

[From the N. O. Tribune of Nov. 8th and 9th.]

BREAKING OF A BALLOT BOX.

We had, last night, the pleasure to see in our office Mr. John Johnson, a very active friend of our cause in the Parish of Assumption, who had to flee, on Monday, to this city, to avoid persecution.

From the information given us by that reliable gentleman, it appears that the military authorities at Napoleonville, banded together with the civil officers, took upon themselves to interfere, in the most brutal manner, with the private affairs of the Republicans of that parish.

On election day, at about 10 o'clock in the morning, the sheriff, O. Melancón, and a squad of cavalrymen went to our poll at Napoleonville, took forcible possession of the ballot-box, broke it open, scattered the tickets they found therein, and carried away a sum of $80, amount of voluntary contributions by the voters, collected during the morning.

Messrs. Eudaldo Pintado and Peter Hills, two well-known Republicans of that place, who were seen at the poll by the invaders, were arrested by order of a colonel and brought to jail, where they were still when our informant, Mr. John Johnson, left the village in great haste to avoid a similar fate.

The sheriff of that parish, who has brought so unenviable notoriety upon his name by such an unwarranted act of violence, is one of the signers of the Ordinance of Secession, and when the Federal forces took possession of Napoleonville, he fled to the so-called Confederate States, where he remained, attending to his private speculations, until the war was over. When Kirby Smith's army surrendered, Mr. O. Maloncón returned to his native place; but on his way thither he had to pass through this city, and called upon Mr. Wells. As soon as our kind Governor was told how sound a secessionist that person was, he appointed him at once sheriff of the parish. As for the colonel who so recklessly exceeded his authority by doing at Napoleonville what Major Generals Sheridan, Canby, T.W. Sherman, O.O. Howard and Fullerton did not think proper to do in this city, when our colored fellow-citizens went openly and in broad daylight to No. 49 Union street to bring in their contributions to our fund, or when they went to vote on Monday, his name is, if we mistake not, Selles, and he commands the 3rd Rhode Island Cavalry regiment. More than once he has expressed his intention to settle in that parish as soon as his regiment is mustered out of service, and devote his time to the legal profession. That may account for his excessive partiality for the copperheads of the place.

The other polls were closed by military order in the same parish; and we are informed that 670 votes were already polled at that early hour, when the mass of the colored citizens, rather than resort to force in defense of their rights, as they might have thought it justifiable to do, concluded not to proceed with their election, and dispersed quietly.

H. C. WARMOTH AND THE LEGAL POLLS.

A great many votes were cast on Monday at the legal polls, in behalf of H. C. Warmoth, for Congress. Judge Warmoth was voted for by the Republicans in all congressional districts, but no official return was furnished of the votes which were cast for him. We can, however, estimate the Republican vote in the Parish of Orleans:

Total vote cast	9,800
Allen and Wells together	7,500
Balance for Warmoth	2,800

We never heard before of returns being truncated, to the detriment of one of the candidates. But everything is *fair* play against the "negroes."

MORE OUTRAGES.

No polls were permitted in Covington for the disfranchised. This is another proof of the loyalty of Louisiana, and also another reason why we should continue to insist claiming the right of representation with taxation, and not as our friends who have just returned from a four years' crusade against Justice and Humanity would have us to accept, as we have always done, namely: to be taxed for the support of their schools and other institutions of the State, and still have no voice in the disposition of the money drawn from us.

We learn that the commissioners of the Parish of St. John the Baptist, who had brought the returns to this city, Messrs. D. Burel and Cephes were arrested, upon a frivolous charge, by the police of New Orleans, when about to leave this place. The arrest took place about eleven o'clock yesterday morning. We will be able to give more information on this new act of persecution in our next issue.

As to the arrests in the Parish of Assumption, we received yesterday from one of the accused, Mr. Eudaldo Pintado, late member of the Convention, the following letter, which speaks for itself:

NAPOLEONVILLE,
in the jail of the Parish of Assumption,
November 7th, 1865.

Messrs. the Editors of the New Orleans Tribune:
Please have the kindness to report to the Central Committee that yesterday morning, while I was in the discharge of my duties as commissioner of election for this parish, I was arrested by order from headquarters at Napoleonville, in consequence of a report made by several rebels of this place, who made the charge of having enticed the freedmen away from their employers, against me as well as other persons who were acting with me as commissioners, and are now imprisoned with me.

I would like to know whether these men had a right to act as they did; and if they had not, I beg of you to take that affair in your charge, for if we stay here much longer we will be reduced to the condition of skeletons and eaten up by vermin; for since we were arrested we could get only a dozen biscuits, full of maggots, for four of us to feed upon. Is that the treatment in reserve for men devoted to the Union, and whose wrong is to advocate a righteous cause?

48

Please inform immediately our friend, Mr. Gallup, that he may procure a counsel for us, for we have none to expect from the persons hereabout, our persecutors being nothing but rebels, and one of the first among them the sheriff, one of the signers of the Ordinance of Secession.

49

Yours, etc., etc.
E. G. PINTADO.

VOLUNTARY ELECTION — THE LATEST RETURNS.

The election has been prevented, by means of intimidation, in the parishes of Lafourche and St. Tammany. However, in the last named, polls were open in Madisonville, where 136 votes were cast for H. C. Warmoth.

APPENDIX.

New Outrages and Persecutions.

After the ridiculous and unwarrantable arrest, in this city, of the two citizens who brought here the returns of the voluntary election for the parish of St. John the Baptist we do not wonder at hearing that the persecution against these gentlemen is still going on. On Sunday afternoon, Messrs. Dan. Burel and William Smith were arrested at Bonnet Carre, by a deputy sheriff, it is said, and taken to the parish jail.

The charge is, as before, a frivolous one — an illegal one — a mere persecution. Lieutenant Rich, the Provost Marshal, has done all in his power to discourage the voluntary election, and, therefore, cannot be expected to do complete justice to our friends.

This renewal of a persecution, which has to terminate, sooner or later. to the confusion of its promoters and agents, has something mean and even puerile. We would rather like to meet the rebels again on the battle-field like men.

We recommend the investigation of this case to the Sub-Committee of the Central Executive Board.

From the New Orleans Tribune; of Nov. 14.

The Republican Meeting Last Night.

In spite of the bad weather we had yesterday, the Republican meeting held last night at the Orleans Theatre, was very well attended. We noticed in the house an unusual array of ladies and an uncommon mixture of white citizens. A good brass band discoursed for some time popular tunes amidst the cheers of the audience, and when the clock struck seven, the curtain rose and Mr. Crane opened the meeting by proposing the Hon. B. F. Flanders for

President. That gentleman was warmly welcomed with applause, when he took his seat.

The following list of Vice Presidents and Secretaries was then read;

VICE-PRESIDENTS — Hon. Anthony Fernandez, Hon. Charles Smith, Hon. E. Hiestand, Hon. T. J. Durant, William H. Higgins, G. W. Breckinridge, Col. C. W. Fox, J. Mohan, B. Rush Plumley, Capt. F. H. Morse, W. R. Harmount, D. C. Woodruff, A Commagere, Ansel Edwards, Thomas H. Bell, Henry C. Dibble, John Page, Henry Train, E. Warren, C. W. Hornor, J. O. Newman, A. W. Lewis, Alfred Jervis, Col. T.B. Thorpe, W. R. Crane, Capt. Henry Stiles, Dr. W. H. Hire, J. L. Imlay, Dr. J. White, Alfred Rougelot, Robert Bennie, Nathan Willey, F. C. Baxter, H. A. Gallup, Thomas Page, Sebastian Seiler, William H. Crawford, Theoden Pincus, B. G. Hank, John Moliere, Dr. J. B. Long, Thomas McRea, F.L. James, William H. Pemberton, James E. Tewel, Thomas E. Ransom, Edward Meyer, L. S. Buchanan, Dr. M. Schuppert, M. L. Block, A. Delage, A. Sarta, Jaimes Mushaway, A. W. Rodgers, F. Marie, Dr. A. Shelley, Joseph Soudé, Noel Bacchus, Othello, Laines, Pierre Canelle, Francois Escoffle, Manuel Moreau, Basile Brion, Arnold Bertaunneau, Laurent August, G. Casnave, Theodore Delassize, E. Dubois, L. Lamaniere, L. Follin, E. Azigg, D. B. Macarty, Vr. Ceressoles, F. C. Cristophe, Ernest Joubert, B. Sanlay, Joseph Curiel, Paul Trevigne, H. Glaudin, Myrtile Coucelle, B. Soulié, Armand Lanusse, H. Camp, Dr. Rondanez, JB. D. Bonseigneur, Charles Aubert, J. B. Noble, R. H. Isabelle, W. C. Johnston, G. Smoot, Dr. W. A. Lewis, Camille Thierry, Blanc Joubert, J. B. Clay, Aristide Mary, Bron Mathe, Edmond Dupuy, Charles Courcelle, L. T. Veissier, Charles Morant, William Lillert, S. H. Rush, George Herriman, A. L. Cheese, A. Latone, F. Xavier, G. P. Dupin, Edmond Rillieux, Henry Bonseigneur, Louis Banks, R. I. Cromwell, John Parsons, John Keppard, E. Carter, Thomas Isabelle, J. H. A. Roberts.

SECRETARIES — J. A. Noble, Charles Montieu, Oscar J. Dunn.

THE REPUBLICAN PARTY — MASS MEETING AT THE ORLEANS THEATRE — SPEECHES BY B. F. FLANDERS, RUFUS WAPLES AND H. C. WARMOTH.

According to announcement, a mass meeting of the Republican party was held last evening at the Orleans Theatre. The audience was large, two-thirds of which was of the colored population.

Agreeably to our custom, we give an impartial report of the speeches made on the occasion, premising that neither a list of the vice-presidents nor a copy of the resolutions were furnished us.

Mr. Crane stepped forward, and stating the object of the meeting, read a list of president and vice-presidents, that were elected officers of the meeting by acclamation.

Mr. B.F. Flanders, the President, then addressed the assemblage in the following words:

I had not prepared a speech, nor did I expect to address you this evening. I expect simply to preside. I am content to act as chairman in the introduction of other speakers, who will address you on this occasion.

Perhaps it may be necessary that should speak to you upon the nature of the Republican party — the Union party of Louisiana. When the rebellion collapsed, when the rebels came back among us and desired to renew their citizenship, we gladly received them.

The people of the United States were willing to accept their protestations. Taking their protestations of willingness to live under the Constitution and the laws the people accepted them once more. They enter the State, they take possession, and close by slamming the doors at the face of Union men, and of men who have never manifested any other feeling than that of loyalty.

Instead of maintaining a spirit of good will, they have denied their offices to Union men. In their nominations, not one loyal man, not one with any pretensions to loyalty, was received, with the exception of their candidate for Governor, and he was brought over with the prospect of obtaining the position. Jacob Barker — I suppose there is no doubt of his loyalty — is, perhaps, another exception. Saving these two, I do not know of any other loyal man upon their ticket.

This must have been either because the Democratic party trusted no loyal man, or that no loyal man trusted the Democratic party. After they had taken possession of the house; after they had slammed the door, finding one or two men who still claimed to be loyal inside, the windows and the doors were suddenly opened, and they were thrown out, heels over head — kicked out. Nay, they boast that in a short time they will kick out the Governor himself.

The views of the Republican party are clear. They represent equal rights before the law. We hear it stated that the men of this party — they who are the advocates of equal rights — will yet be killed upon the streets — that it will be unsafe for them to hold their opinions. This threat has been held out to us that the Union men are to be killed. (Cries of never, never.) Now, some of us may fall. If we cannot discuss our principles without fear of assassination, we may know it. Whatever the Democratic party here may advocate, they of the North are irrevocably wedded to this doctrine, the right of free speech and a free press.

I counsel patience and forbearance to you all; to patiently bear the wrongs, the insults to which you are subjected. I would have you guilty of no indiscreet act of violence or outrage. Let us bear and suffer wrongs, for to act in a hasty manner is what our opponents desire.

Mr. Flanders closed his remarks in counselling the colored people to go on as they had previously been doing, the firm, the steady advocates of equality before the law.

On the close of the speech, Mr. Flanders introduced Rufus Waples to the audience, who was received with loud cheering.

SPEECH OF RUFUS WAPLES.

Mr. President, Gentlemen and Fellow-Citizens:
It is a great privilege, as well as a great responsibility, to address such a crowd of honest men upon the topics of the day. I feel that the welcome given to me was not for me alone, but for the people's cause I plead. I regret we have not here the Honorable Senator Yates, of Illinois, nor that noble tribune of the people, Thomas J. Durant.

Here the speaker mapped out his intentions, in saying, though he would call things by their right names, yet he would endeavor to give offense to none. He did not indulge in invective, nor was it his policy to give acrimonious words. If he thrust an arrow in the beast of an opponent, he was welcome to thrust it back again.

If I use the term rebel, it is because the man has revolted against his country. If I use the term traitor, it is in the constitutional sense. If I use the term rebellion, it is because no other word can fit or express the hellish character of the thing.

In the late election held in our midst, one was legal, the other voluntary. One half of the one was made up of the disloyal, the other held by those whose every bone was loyal to the United States. One of them was composed of men who still walk the streets and fight their battles over again, boasting triumphs over the Federal arms. The other is composed of men who are calmly and dispassionately viewing the results of things, with no other object in view than to petition Congress for relief. One of them supported men of well known Confederate proclivities, the other our noble standard bearer, H. C. Warmoth.

Warmoth the soldier; the man who organized the first regiment of Missouri militia outside of St. Louis, early in the day, before the fall of Fort Sumter, and who served with it till after the bloody battle of Wilson's Creek, where it was so badly cut up that it was afterwards consolidated with another regiment. You have elected *Colonel* Warmoth, who led the 32nd Missouri Volunteers (another regiment organized by himself) at the battle of Chickasaw Bayou, under the since glorious Sherman; and, as a staff officer, under General McClernand; served with the Thirteenth Army Corps at the battles of Port Gibson, Champion Hill, Big Black Bridge, the charge of the 19th May on the enemy's works at Vicksburg, and also on the 22nd, when he was severely wounded and disabled. You have elected one who subsequently led his regiment, under old fighting Joe Hooker, to the top of Lookout Mountain, to make the charge on Missionary Ridge, as he did, on the following day, capturing prisoners, artillery and hundreds of small arms. You have elected one who has served you nearer home, at Alexandria and on the Texas coast — always with honor and distinction. You have elected *Brig. General* Warmoth, for he enjoyed that title while in command of six thousand militia here in 1863, and resigned it for active service in the field; but you know once a general always a general. You have elected *Judge* Warmoth, who served here acceptably upon the bench, where his legal and military knowledge were both called into requisition as Provost Judge. How eloquent is this simple history! How sublime the unadorned narrative! He did not "fight his battles o'er again" as the rebel candidates did during the late canvass; he pleaded your cause and not his own. His nomination as a candidate was without solicitation on his part, for I happen to know that he sought others to get them to allow their names as candidates in preference to his own. It may be said to him as was said to George Washington in the Virginia House of Delegates, when he, a young Colonel had just returned from his perilous expedition to Fort Duquesne, "Your modesty alone is equal to your merits." You have made him more than colonel, brigadier, provost judge, the rising lawyer, the popular orator, for you made him the delegate of a free constituency to the most important legislative body on earth. You have practically demonstrated that the territory of Louisiana can send a delegate to Congress, and that colored men are capable of voting.

On this the speaker alluded to the construction of the State, in which he advocated that the State Government had been destroyed. He spoke as follows:

I set out with the proposition *that the State Government of Louisiana has been destroyed*. It is impossible to conceive of a *State*, in the sense in which States are known to the Federal Constitution, unless the following three essential elements are combined:

1. Land, or space for inhabitants.

2. A Constitution not repugnant to the Federal Constitution.

3 Citizenship such as the Federal Constitution requires.

The first element, land, has never been wanting. But the second has failed. The people met 1n convention in 1861 and struck out the requirement obliging officers to swear allegiance to the United States of America and the State of Louisiana, and inserted "the Confederate States of America and the State of Louisiana." They made the instrument repugnant to the Federal Constitution. From that moment one of the essential ingredients of a State Government, under our system, was wanting, and the State ceased to exist.

They treated Louisiana as if she were a separate nationality; it is a fatal principle that has misled hundreds of men. The Convention of 1861 met there for the purpose of tinkering with the Constitution of 1852. They did change. They did make a Constitution repugnant to the Constitution of the United States. From that very moment Louisiana ceased to be a State.

The third element also proved wanting. When the people met in Constitutional Convention and made their organic law repugnant, they gave evidence that the citizenship of Louisiana was not loyal — not such as the Federal Constitution required. They gave similar evidence when they adopted that absolute nullity, the secession ordinance. They gave similar evidence when they levied war against the United States and adhered to the enemy, giving him aid and comfort.

Thus two of the essentials to a State Government under the Constitution of the United States, have proved wanting, and it follows that the State was destroyed.

Every department of the Federal Government has acted upon this doctrine, whether it will acknowledge it now or not. Congress has declared the rebellious *States* in insurrection as well as the inhabitants of those States; has passed laws distinguishing loyal from disloyal States; providing for the collection of taxes in "the insurrectionary districts," voting men and money to subdue the rebellious citizens of the Republic inhabiting those insurrectionary districts; thus treating them as wanting in the two essential elements last named.

The Executive has approved all of these acts; has issued several proclamations declaring the existence of the insurrection; has spoken of the State Governments as subverted, disorganized, disconstructed, (for he has spoken of the contemplated "restoration, " "reorganization," and "reconstruction" of the rebellious districts) and he has, as Commander-in-Chief of the Army and Navy, prosecuted a war of defense in opposition to insurgents, because they were not such citizens as the Constitution requires.

The Supreme Court has said that the rebellious States organized war in their State capacity, thus acknowledging that they were not such organizations as the Federal Constitution requires. The Supreme Court has further said that the rebel territory, bounded by lines of bayonets, was well defined, and that the United States possessed the same belligerent rights against them that they would possess against a foreign foe. (2 Black, S.C. Reports.) They go on further to notice the fact that these rebellious States formed alliances among themselves; and we know that no State can do this without making itself repugnant to the supreme law of the land. Hardly any act has been done by any one of the three departments of the Government which has not been in harmony with the theory that the rebel States had destroyed their own existence, and in perfect discord with the opposite theory. The appointment of Provisional Governors can be justified on no other theory.

Who contends that President Johnson can legally appoint a Provisional Governor for the State of Massachusetts? A Provisional Governor is a civil officer — because the functions which he performs are civil. He is the Governor of a territory. The Constitution does not fix the name by which such officers are to be called, and there is nothing in a name. In the exercise of their functions, they are Governors of territories and act as such. Look at our restrictions upon trade — our "acting collectors," etc. — our limited privileges; do you tell me that this is the result of invidious legislation? If Louisiana is a State like Massachusetts, why this distinction? "O, these were war measures," you say. Yes, and the war was made by rebel organizations, which were the remains of former States — and that is the true reason of this legislation, which was quite proper for that condition of things, but which would have been highly improper had Louisiana and her confederates remained States, *i.e.,* organizations with loyal citizenship and right constitutions.

Mr. Waples then proceeded to say that it was not impossible for a State to destroy its own existence, and labored to prove it. He imagined the people all to emigrate, when it would cease to be a State, and further said the people might prefer no State government and live like they of the District of Columbia. He referred to the objection that though we may grant a State may destroy itself, the action was illegal, so far as Louisiana was concerned. In answering this he held that though the action might be illegal, yet legal consequences flow from illegal acts, instancing the illegal act of confinement made of Rougelot and Bennie, who were cast into prison for saying colored men had a right to vote, but legal consequences may be visited on the heads of their persecutors.

It was illegal for Messrs. Pintado and Hills, Commissioners of Election in Assumption parish, to be handcuffed and imprisoned for performing their duties; but legal consequences of the most momentous character must follow such an outrage. Kill a man, see his dead body before you, and will you deny the fact that he is dead, merely because he was not legally killed? Will you deny that the widow does not acquire right to her community property? It was wrong to make the Constitution of Louisiana repugnant to the Federal Constitution; it was wrong for the people of Louisiana to begin insurrection; but the legal consequence is — the State has ceased to be.

But here comes another objector — and he comes like Bildad, in the Book of Job "with his belly full of arguments." He says, "I don't believe in secession, and therefore the States did not go out, and they must still be in the Union." I agree with you that the ordinance of secession was an absolute nullity. and that the States did not, in fact or in law, secede from the Union; that they are still, and have ever continued to be, component parts of the Republic. While a State may throw off its own government, it cannot divest the Federal Government of its jurisdiction.

Louisiana is a territory under the exclusive jurisdiction of the Federal Government. Had she seceded, she, being an independent nation, would have been under her State government only. But, as she was not a nation, and could not secede, the only effect of the destruction of her State government is to leave the other government, the Federal, ruling alone. The allegiance of the people of Louisiana to the United States remains intact. The land remains and is a part of the territory of the great Republic — territory which stretches from ocean to ocean, partly organized, partly unorganized, and partly disorganized. Louisiana belongs to the last named description in one sense, and to the first named in another. Louisiana has an organization, but it is not a legal State organization — nor is it exactly similar to our usual territorial organization. Nevertheless, it may be correctly styled a territorial organization. There is no definite method for forming territorial governments, nor is there any prescribed form. Congress may pass enabling acts or not — it is immaterial. The Constitution is almost silent on the subject. The Governors may be called "Provisional Governors," just as well as by any other name. The legislatures may legislate, and the courts may do business under the old style — "the State of Louisiana," just as well as not.

The people of this territory have a right to send a delegate to Congress. Forming a part of this nation, they ought to be heard. Other territories send delegates, and why should not this send one? Nevada has just elected a delegate. It is vain to urge that Congress has not passed an enabling act, for there is no Constitutional provision requiring it. The people are competent to act without it, especially when they already have an organization, existing *ex necessitate*. Congress is competent to receive a delegate from any sort of a territory, whether organized or unorganized, or disorganized —whether there was a previous enabling act or not for there is no constitutional prohibition, and there are no constitutional implications. There is just as much law for receiving a delegate from Louisiana as there is for receiving one from Nevada. Of course, the delegate must be legally chosen — chosen by the people — by the *whole* people. All who are citizens of the United States, all of whom the Government claims allegiance, who are of the pro per age and sex, must have the opportunity of assisting in the selection of the delegate. So selected, it is the duty of Congress to receive him; to allow him to participate in the discussion, and to give him all the rights of a territorial delegate.

I will here leave the line of my argument for a moment to congratulate you upon the exercise of this right in the election of H.C. Warmoth, Esq. You demonstrated the truth that it is practicable to hold an election where the citizens heretofore disfranchised could vote. Two years ago it was said that negroes could not make soldiers they whipped their enemies, and now nobody doubts that they can fight. A month ago it was said that they could not make voters; they have succeeded orderly and intelligently at the ballot-box, and now who shall say that they are incapable of voting? The world moves. The most ignorant laborer in the sugar fields, with the longest heel and the flatest nose, is a better voter today than John Slidell was in his palmiest days of power. The negroes are all educated — educated in the school of experience, and in suffering and wrong — educated to hate slavery, and to hate treason, its naturally begotten off spring. They voted for no traitor on Monday last; they elected a loyal man.

To my fourth proposition:

The work of adopting a form of State Government, and petitioning Congress for admission, belongs to the people of the territory, to the whole people, and to them only.

The central idea of our American system the grand axiom on which our National Constitution rests, *Governments derive their just powers from the consent of the governed*, applied to State as well as to the Federal Government. This is the leading idea of the Declaration of Independence. All that goes before and all that comes after it, is subsidiary. This was *the idea* of the Revolutionary War, in opposition to the monarchical idea that the King rules by divine right. This was *the idea* of the late war of deleuse against those who held the monarchical doctrine that the ample derive their powers and privileges from government, *i.e.*, the crown. It is a doctrine of universal application — it applies to the "governed" in Louisiana. On this rock I rest my proposition.

The work belongs to *the whole people* of Louisiana. As the colored men have equal rights before the law in the territories of the United States; and equal rights by natural law, everywhere; as they are a part of "the governed," they must have a hand in the work. Any organization made without their consent cannot have "just powers;" cannot be such an organization as Congress would be justified in receiving. It must have the consent of the majority of the whole, white and black.

The fatal objections to the present form of government, adopted by the late Louisiana Convention, are, that the voice of the whole loyal people was not heard – that it is not republican, and that there was undue interference on the part of the National Government. Had this form originated with the whole loyal people, without dictation from the Federal Government, we might have gone with it in our hands as a part of our petition, and asked admission as a State. But Congress would have been in duty bound to refuse, because the form is anti-republican, since it excludes a large majority of the loyal men from the suffrage.

The now much talked of plan of reconstruction is manifestly illegal, because it proposes a royal road for the admission of States, unknown to the Federal Constitution. The defunct States cannot be galvanized into life. Their relations to the Federal Government are not better than those of Utah and Nevada, as we have already seen. Neither the President nor Congress can create State governments. It is fallacious to say that they can remove the disabilities, for that is only another form of saying that they can re-create the lost States.

If they are now States, they were such throughout the war. Louisiana was such at the opening of Congress in December, 1861, and might have legally had Senators and Representatives there. Imagine the insurrectionary "States" (so called) fighting the Government on the field, and yet voting in the United States Congress on war questions refusing to grant supplies refusing to pay the army; refusing to support the Government! Then tell me that this is all legal! What monstrous absurdity! And yet this reconstruction plan embraces just this absurdity!

It is not precisely correct to say that we owe paramount allegiance to the General Government. We owe *exclusive* allegiance to that Government in all matters within its powers, and *exclusive* allegiance to our State Government (when we have one) in all matters within its powers.

If I have established my fourth proposition, I have proved already that the President cannot by proclamation that the rebel State Governments are restored, render it the duty of the Clerk of the House to place the representatives from such so-called States upon the roll. If the people can only create them, subject to admission by Congress as new States, the President cannot do it.

THE POLITICAL REGENERATION OF THE STATE IS INEXPEDIENT NOW.

The present condition of society is unfavorable to wise and harmonious action. The recent election shows that the white Union men are very much in the minority here. A State organized now would be made by the white majority, and be actuated still by the spirit with which they acknowledge to have inaugurated the war. Their public speakers and candidates fought their Confederate battles over again in their speeches, and gloried in victories achieved over Union arms. They were elected by immense majorities. Men opposed to Republican State government have been returned to Congress as the result of this mockery of an election. It is, therefore, inexpedient to attempt the making of a new State by white voters.

It is true, counting all the voters, white and black, the majority is favorable to Republican government but the temper of the unrepentant traitors renders good men apprehensive that they would, by violence, undertake to defeat the will of the majority. War ought to be avoided. The Union men were persecuted at the election on Monday last, but they in patience wait, believing that all will be well, and hoping in Congress.

Another reason why action is impolitic now is, that we have no assurance that the work would be permanent. There is danger that, under the name of

State rights, the strong would trample upon the weak, as before the war; the action of the majority would be disregarded, and might would trample over right. A constitution adopted now, might be repealed next year, and an aristocratic instrument substituted. We had better wait till time has cooled the temper of these Hotspurs; till reflection shall have brought them to properly estimate the sanctity of their oaths of allegiance till candid investigation shall have proved an antidote to the prejudice existing against the loyal colored men, as it has, to a great degree, removed the prejudice formerly existing against the Jews, the Quakers, and others who are remarkable for singularity of physiognomy, dress or complexion. If it should take ten years to prepare the public mind to petition for admission into the Union, with a Republican Constitution, that is a short time in the life of a great nation like ours but two years of waiting would work wonders. Let neither South Carolina nor Louisiana have occasion hereafter to say that she was held in the Union against their will. Thus shall Union and liberty be perpetuated.

PREAMBLES AND RESOLUTIONS ADOPTED AT THE REPUBLICAN MEETING.

The following are the preambles and resolutions adopted by said meeting, and which have only been published in substance in the N. O. Times:

Whereas, at the election held in this city and in the parishes, on Monday last, the 6th inst., the Republican party of Louisiana was triumphant, electing Judge H.C. Warmoth as our delegate to Congress by 19, 000 votes; and

Whereas, the vote would have been very much larger, if not doubled, but for the interference of men, late traitors, and of others, who broke up the ballot boxes and arrested the commissioners of the election in one parish, and impeded and prevented the election in other parishes; and

Whereas, our honored standard-bearer, Judge Warmoth is about to depart to the capital of the country, there to represent us, and the principles of our platform in the Congress of the nation, therefore, as an expression of our opinions and purposes:

1. *Be it resolved*, That the wanton, tyrannical and cruel interference with the free people of Louisiana, assembling peaceably to express their sentiments

by ballot, is another evidence of the unfitness of the rebel majority of white men in Louisiana to administer justly the government thereof.

2. *Resolved*, that there can be no "State," in the sense implied by the Federal Constitution, without a loyal organization in said State.

3. *Resolved*, that the State organization of Louisiana was made "repugnant" to the Federal Constitution by the alteration made in said State organization by the Convention of 1861; that the subsequent attempt to form a new Constitution is null and of no effect, because the new State Government, so called, did not derive its powers from the consent of the governed.

4. *Resolved*, that we are without any duly authorized State Government in Louisiana; that we are in a territorial condition, under the exclusive jurisdiction of the Federal Government.

5. *Resolved*, that the State Government having been made repugnant to the Federal Constitution, both in law and in fact, and therefore overthrown to all intents and purposes, that the President of the United States cannot restore it by proclamation.

6. *Resolved*, that the State can only be restored in the constitutional way, by petitioning Congress for admission whenever a majority of the whole people deem it expedient to so petition.

7. *Resolved*, that the temper of a majority of the white voters, nine-tenths of whom are disloyal, renders it inexpedient to apply at this time for admission, and unsafe for Congress to admit us.

8. *Resolved*, that even in face of these conditions, in Louisiana, we rejoice with the Republican party everywhere, over the recent triumph of Republican principles in the Northern elections, from which triumph we hope for strength and ultimate success in Louisiana.

9. *Resolved*, that our hope is in Congress. That the premature admission of senators and representatives from Louisiana would be disastrous to the loyal people here. It would place us under rebel rule, under the control of men who are today as malignant toward the Union and Union men as upon any day of the late Confederacy.   10. *Resolved*, that, as loyal citizens, we will resort to all peaceable means for the redress of our grievances and for the securing of our right to life, liberty and the pursuit of happiness.

11. *Resolved*, that the experiment of "reconstructing" Louisiana by the hands that late were rebel, and red with the blood of loyal men, has failed, as

it should, being unjust to the loyal men, dead and living, and to the few Confederates who have taken the oath in good faith.

12. *Resolved*, that we denounce as false and calumnious the charge made by J. Madison Wells, and reiterated by the journals of this city, that the men who voted at the "polls of the disfranchised," on Monday, the 6th of November, for a delegate to represent us at Washington were required to pay one dollar, or any other sum of money, before being allowed to vote.

13. *Resolved*, that we denounce as outrageous the act of the commissioners of elections, in the late election, in refusing the right to vote to white Federal soldiers of the First New Orleans Regiment of Infantry, who were duly qualified according to law said refusal being unwarranted by law, unjust to the soldiers of the Republic, and rife with the spirit of the late rebellion from which the officers of said election were largely gathered.

14. *Resolved*, that we denounce the registration of returned rebel soldiers, and the reception and counting of their votes at the last election, as contrary to the proclamation of the President and the decision of the Attorney General; which decision declares that such men have lost their residence by absence, and can only vote after one year's sojourn in the State.

15. *Resolved*, that we, loyal men of Louisiana, have full confidence in our delegate to Congress, Hon. Judge H. C. Warmoth that his loyalty, courage and ability have been tried on the battle fields for the Nation's life, and have been shown in the integrity and devotion of his civil and political career.

We do therefore commend him heartily to all men who love liberty and justice.

Judge Warmoth, the delegate elect, was then introduced to the audience, who received him with enthusiasm. He thanked his fellow-citizens who had so unanimously honored him with their suffrages on Monday last, and said he should regard his election as the proudest achievement of his life, if he should live to be a thousand years old. He promised to represent his constituents to the best of his ability, and warned them that the disloyalists were doing all in their power to secure their ends, representing the black man as degraded and ignorant. It was said that the Yankee did not know anything about the negro; but he would tell them that the Yankee knew everything — all about this war and how it would end. They had invented the telegraph which had just informed them that New Jersey had come back into the Union, and were inventing new machines every day; and when he went North, it was his intention to try to get a Yankee to invent a machine to pump out their black blood and pump in white blood. [Laughter and applause] There would be no trouble then about their voting, for all they would have to do would be to wash their faces and go to the ballot-box. [Continued laughter.] But the real trouble was not that they were black, ignorant and degraded. but that they would not vote the Democratic ticket.

It was charged that they would not work. If there was anything he didn't like to do it was to work. Work in this country was unnecessary, as soil and climate produced a living almost spontaneously. He had been elected by a handsome majority, and supposed it was the part of magnanimity to say nothing about his opponent, but he was really sorry for his friend Col. Field, who had been very badly beaten. He was the hind horse in the whole race, and had held on to that thing "Conservative" too long. The election was over but their work was not done; they had only taken one step in the great tragedy which was yet to be enacted. The impression created in the Southern mind against them could not easily be removed, and he expected assistance at their hands. They must send their delegates to Washington — white and colored — and let the people know in the South that the negro population of this city is not the ignorant and degraded people they are represented to be. [Applause.] They could not remove these impressions and prejudices by simply writing letters. They must send their best, smartest and most intelligent men, if they would succeed, for there was no disguising the fact that the mind of the people of the North as well as elsewhere was prejudiced against them. If they had worked as hard as their opponents, they would have had a Provisional Governor in this State a month ago. Governor Wells occupied his position by their own neglect. When they found that he had sold out the State they should have gone to Washington and urged upon the President his removal and the appointment of a loyal man. [Applause.] He continued to urge the sending of delegates to the capital, and closed as follows: Fellow-citizens, I thank you for your attention, and I feel happy tonight because I am going home; that is, I am going where I used to call home before I came down here —going to see my friends, and tell them in a plain, common sense way all about you, what kind of people you are, how clever to me; and I know that statement will go right straight to their hearts. I will tell them of your loyalty and enthusiasm for the Government; that you are the only people who love the Republic, and sing the songs of the Union and wave the flag; that the rebels hate the flag, and do not love the Republic, and sing only one song, and that is Dixie. When I shall have come back I hope I shall be able to say that I did my duty, and succeeded in the great enterprise which we all have at heart. [Applause.]

At the conclusion of his speech, Judge Warmoth was presented with a handsome bouquet by the Rev. Mr. Baylor, a colored clergyman.

The meeting then adjourned.

[From the New Orleans Times of November 15th.]

TREASON AGAINST THE PEOPLE AND THE LAWS.

In our edition of yesterday we gave a full report of the proceedings had and speeches delivered at the radical meeting held on the previous evening at the old Orleans Theatre. In doing so we performed what we conceived to be our duty as a public journalist, which was at the first and still is — "to hold, as 'twere, the mirror up to nature;" — but our action in the premises must by no means be considered as an endorsement of the views and sentiments of the speakers.

Benjamin F; Flanders, the President of the grand motley ratification gathering, and Rufus Waples, the principal orator, are gentlemen who have been pre-eminently distinguished for their loyalty; while others have suffered by the war, they have been so fortunate as to greatly increase their worldly goods. Such immense rewards for such limited services as they rendered should have taught them generosity, but it has not done so. They seem to fear an interruption of the golden tide which made the losses of their neighbors a gain to them, and with such arms of rebellion as they dare to raise, they now oppose the Constitution of the United States and the policy of the President, who has sworn to support it. Some may suppose that we are prejudiced against them. Not so. With something of sorrow, but without a particle of malice, we appeal "to the law and the testimony" in the premises.

Inferentially and almost directly, Mr. Flanders charges nine-tenths of the white population of Louisiana with perjury by taking an oath of allegiance they did not intend to keep. He charges them with disloyalty; with slamming the door in the face of Unionism with nominating for the late election only disloyal men barely excepting the Governor, whom they, he says. intend to kick out as soon as possible, and Jacob Barker, in whom Mr. F. has but little faith: More than all this, Mr. Flanders insinuates that those who acted with the successful party in the late election in this city have uttered threats of assassination against "the Union men" — a title which he arrogates to himself and his peculiar friends.

And this address, it must be remembered, is delivered in the city of New Orleans, to an audience of recently emancipated negroes, who receive the utterances of the crater with wild shouts of approval and cries of "never! never!" Though sensitive, our people are long-suffering. They may look on incendiary doctrines and the teachers thereof with contempt, for they have determined to leave their vindication, under the repeated insults heaped upon them by the demagogues of a fanatic guild, to time and the sovereignty of law.

No man knows better than Mr. Flanders that the people of Louisiana are today as loyal to the Union as those of Connecticut or Maine. Anyone who would speak against the Union now would be regarded as insane, and to utter threats against a man because of his Unionism, would be the extreme of madness. But a man may be sound as to the Union and unsound as to other things. The Union must not be held up as a cloak for the incendiary and assassin, and a disbelief in incendiarism cannot be put forward by even the most ingenious demagogue as sufficient grounds for such grave charges as perjury and treason.

The address of Mr. Waples is characteristic and peculiar, especially when it is remembered that the speaker was recently a law officer of the Government. There seems to be a vein of vindictiveness in the course of his argument; a malicious delight in giving trouble to an Administration that, for some unexplained reason, had dispensed with his valuable services. In opposition to the greatest statesmen of our age and nation, and in violation of the plainest principles of common sense, Mr. Waples contends that, though the ordinance of secession was an absolute nullity, yet by it Louisiana lost her status as a State, and sank back into a territorial condition. He insists on the grand American axiom that "governments derive their just powers from the consent of the governed," and then claims as a legitimate deduction that as the negro is to be governed, he must of necessity be a citizen and voter. Hear him:

The work belongs to the *whole people* of Louisiana. As the colored men have equal rights before the law in the territories of the United States; and equal rights, by natural law, everywhere; as they are a part of "the governed," they must have a hand in the work. Any organization made without their consent cannot have "just powers" cannot be such an organization as Congress would be justifiable in receiving. It must have the consent of the majority of the whole, white and black.

It follows, according to the position here laid down, that the Government of the United States has thus far been a Government of fraud, for it has never recognized the negroes any more than the Indians as citizens that not a single State of the Union has had "just powers" conferred upon it. It is strange, indeed, that so penetrating a lawyer could have ever been loyal to such a Government — a Government without "*just powers.*"

But a truce to the farce of a negro election and to the eulogies pronounced on the negro-elected delegate to Congress. Mr. Waples knows well that Louisiana is not in a territorial condition; that the negroes are not citizens; that the pretended election of Mr. Warmoth is a ridiculous farce, and that the incendiary addresses delivered at such meetings are certain to have a most mischievous effect. He knows, moreover, that the highest judicial powers of the Government have pronounced upon the negro's status, and that the highest Executive power of the Government has recognized all the States as in the Union. It is, therefore; treason against our entire population, as well as against the law, to attempt to deceive the negro by a solemn electoral farce to sow the seeds of increased bitterness between the two races in the South, and to oppose the Government in its holy work of restoring harmony to a long distracted land!

[From the New Orleans Tribune of November 15th.]

INTERESTING DOCUMENTS — CHARGE OF JUDGE ABELL TO THE GRAND JURY — INTERESTING REMARKS OF THE SOUTHERN STAR.

Judge Abell has always been known as a strong pro-slavery man. A member of the Convention of 1864, he refused to sign that instrument by which Louisiana was made a free State. The following quotation from the charge he rendered day before yesterday, will give a fair idea of the partial laws and the arrogant spirit the people of color may expect from the party to which he belongs:

"The good order that prevailed throughout Monday last, the day of our general election, indicates a law-abiding disposition, worthy to be made an example for all time to come. (This remark will apply well to the colored citizens who polled 19,000 votes at their voluntary election on the same day.) The decided manner in which the people express their preference for Democratic principles, the intelligence and worth of those selected to carry them out, gives promise to the State that she will be redeemed from the condition into which she has been plunged by violence and corruption. Were it not for the early convening of the General Assemblies, I would deem it my duty to call your attention to grave and important matters, concerning, the good order and police of the parish and State, particularly to the first section of an act of the General Assembly; approved 14th of March, 1830, relative to creating discontent among the colored people of the State, the provisions of which are so salutary to the best interests of the freedman and so terrible to ministers of discontent.

It is to be regretted that some of our fellow-citizens, who have grown up with the State, appear to be so far deluded as in some measure to give their approbation and assistance to a class of adventurers who infest the city and parishes of the State without any occupation except to teach the negroes insubordination to the laws of the State by instructing them that they have a right to vote, etc., which they know to be in direct violation of the laws of the land, which is clearly subversive of good order, productive of discontent among the colored people and endangers the peace of the State.

This class of adventurers are traditionally known to the people of the South, as equally ready to become sympathizers or negro drivers, according to circumstances and the chances of turning a penny. Such treason against the law cannot be tolerated in any community.

The Legislature, I have no doubt, will modify the laws upon this and kindred subjects to suit the changed state of things. The substrata of which will be to furnish the colored people of the State protection of person, property and proceeds of industry, and to teach them the necessary virtue of obedience to the laws, peaceful and respectful conduct as their true and best interest, and the class of white persons referred to, the propriety and justice of remaining at home or engaging in lawful pursuits in the State:

"Gentlemen, the proclamations of the President, and General Orders of the Commanding Generals of this Department, may have so far affected the laws on this subject as perhaps to render it proper to take no action, until the subject has undergone a review by the Legislature. Trusting to your discrimination and zeal for the public good, I will not particularize as to the class of offences that more especially claim your attention."

The *Southern Star* publishes the following remarks on the last Republican meeting. They show the feelings of the rebel press of this city. What will the *Times* —which reported the proceedings — say to the *Star*'s allegation that "no decent paper would give a report of the proceedings." Says the *Southern Star*:

THE NEGRO PEOPLE. — The negro people — white and black — had a meeting last night at the old Orleans Opera House. Some of the talkers at the assemblage will, no doubt, be taken in hand by the Grand Jury of the Parish of Orleans, in accordance with the charge of Judge Abell of the Criminal Court. As a matter of course, we do not report the proceedings — no decent paper would do so. We pity the deluded colored people, and we hope to see their white comrades addressed by Judge Abell — he on the bench and they in the dock.

ABSTRACT OF THE REPORT OF THE COMMITTEE ON ELECTIONS OF THE REPUBLICAN PARTY.

New Orleans, Nov. 16, 1865.

To the Honorable President and members of the Central Executive Committee of the Republican party of Louisiana: — Your Committee to whom was referred the duty of arranging and holding an election on the 6th inst., of the loyal unenfranchised citizens of Louisiana, beg leave to make the following report of the returns received from the following parishes, viz:

Parson of Orleans — 9,044

"	"	Jefferson	2,667
"	"	St. John the Baptist	874
"	"	St. Charles	813
"	"	Ascension	756
"	"	St. James	305
"	"	East Baton Rouge	1,836
"	"	West Baton Rouge	492
"	"	Point Coupée	824
"	"	Terrebonne	1,358
"	"	St. Tammany	136
"	"	St. Helena	247
"	"	St. James	44

19,896

Total number of votes for Judge H. C. Warmoth.

The vote would have, in all probability, been more than doubled were it not for the cowardly interference of our enemies, the planters, who would not allow their hands to vote.

The election was conducted in a perfectly quiet and orderly manner so far as the colored citizens were concerned, and had elections been permitted in all the parishes there is no doubt but the whole number of votes of the loyal unenfranchised citizens would have far outnumbered that of the disloyal enfranchised.

O.J. DUNN, Chairman,
JOS. L. MONTIEU,
W.R. CRANE,
J.L. IMLAY,
RUFUS WAPLES,
Committee on Election.

www.ingramcontent.com/pod-product-compliance
Lightning Source LLC
Chambersburg PA
CBHW030825060726
47590CB00004B/1399